SOME TURNS OF THOUGHT IN
MODERN PHILOSOPHY

LONDON
Cambridge University Press
FETTER LANE

BOMBAY · CALCUTTA · MADRAS
Macmillan

TOKYO
Maruzen Company Ltd

All rights reserved

SOME TURNS OF THOUGHT IN MODERN PHILOSOPHY

Five Essays

BY

GEORGE SANTAYANA

*Published under the auspices of the
Royal Society of Literature*

CAMBRIDGE
AT THE UNIVERSITY PRESS
1933

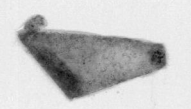

PRINTED IN GREAT BRITAIN

CONTENTS

I. Locke and the Frontiers of Common Sense *page* 1

Paper read before the Royal Society of Literature on the occasion of the Tercentenary of the birth of John Locke. With some Supplementary Notes

II. Fifty Years of British Idealism 48

Reflections on the republication of Bradley's *Ethical Studies*

III. Revolutions in Science 71

Some Comments on the Theory of Relativity and the new Physics

IV. A Long Way Round to Nirvana 87

Development of a suggestion found in Freud's *Beyond the Pleasure Principle*

V. The Prestige of the Infinite 102

A review of Julien Benda's *Sketch of a consistent theory of the relations between God and the World*

The Author's acknowledgments are due to the Editors of *The New Adelphi*, *The Dial*, and the *Journal of Philosophy*, in which one or more of these Essays originally appeared.

I

LOCKE AND THE FRONTIERS OF COMMON SENSE[1]

A GOOD portrait of Locke would require an elaborate background. His is not a figure to stand statuesquely in a void: the pose might not seem grand enough for bronze or marble. Rather he should be painted in the manner of the Dutch masters, in a sunny interior, scrupulously furnished with all the implements of domestic comfort and philosophic enquiry: the Holy Bible open majestically before him, and beside it that other revelation—the terrestrial globe. His hand might be pointing to a microscope set for examining the internal constitution of a beetle: but for the moment his eye should be seen wandering through the open window, to admire the blessings of thrift and liberty manifest in the people so worthily busy in the market-place, wrong as many

[1] Paper read before the Royal Society of Literature on the occasion of the Tercentenary of the birth of John Locke.

a monkish notion might be that still troubled their poor heads. From them his enlarged thoughts would easily pass to the stout carved ships in the river beyond, intrepidly setting sail for the Indies, or for savage America. Yes, he too had travelled, and not only in thought. He knew how many strange nations and false religions lodged in this round earth, itself but a speck in the universe. There were few ingenious authors that he had not perused, or philosophical instruments that he had not, as far as possible, examined and tested; and no man better than he could understand and prize the recent discoveries of "the incomparable Mr Newton". Nevertheless, a certain uneasiness in that spare frame, a certain knitting of the brows in that aquiline countenance, would suggest that in the midst of their earnest eloquence the philosopher's thoughts might sometimes come to a stand. Indeed, the visible scene did not exhaust the complexity of his problem; for there was also what he called "the scene of ideas ", immaterial and private, but often more crowded and pressing than the public scene. Locke was the father of modern psychology, and the birth of this airy monster, this half-natural changeling, was not altogether easy or fortunate.[1]

I wish my erudition allowed me to fill in this picture as the subject deserves, and to trace home the sources of Locke's opinions, and their immense influence. Unfortunately, I can consider him—what is hardly fair—only as a pure philosopher: for had Locke's mind been more profound, it might have been less influential. He was in sympathy with the coming age, and was able to guide it: an age that confided in easy, eloquent reasoning, and proposed to be saved, in this world and the next, with as little philosophy and as little religion as possible. Locke played in the eighteenth century very much the part that fell to Kant in the nineteenth. When quarrelled with, no less than when embraced, his opinions became a point of departure for universal developments. The more we look into the matter, the more we are impressed by the patriarchal dignity of Locke's mind. Father of psychology, father of the criticism of knowledge, father of theoretical liberalism,

[1] See note 1, p. 26.

god-father at least of the American political system, of Voltaire and the Encyclopaedia, at home he was the ancestor of that whole school of polite moderate opinion which can unite liberal Christianity with mechanical science and with psychological idealism. He was invincibly rooted in a prudential morality, in a rationalised Protestantism, in respect for liberty and law: above all he was deeply convinced, as he puts it, "that the handsome conveniences of life are better than nasty penury". Locke still speaks, or spoke until lately, through many a modern mind, when this mind was most sincere; and two hundred years before Queen Victoria he was a Victorian in essence.

A chief element in this modernness of Locke was something that had hardly appeared before in pure philosophy, although common in religion: I mean, the tendency to deny one's own presuppositions—not by accident or inadvertently, but proudly and with an air of triumph. Presuppositions are imposed on all of us by life itself: for instance the presupposition that life is to continue, and that it is worth living. Belief is born on the wing and awakes to many tacit commitments. Afterwards, in reflection, we may wonder at finding these presuppositions on our hands and, being ignorant of the natural causes which have imposed them on the animal mind, we may be offended at them. Their arbitrary and dogmatic character will tempt us to condemn them, and to take for granted that the analysis which undermines them is justified, and will prove fruitful. But this critical assurance in its turn seems to rely on a dubious presupposition, namely, that human opinion must always evolve in a single line, dialectically, providentially, and irresistibly. It is at least conceivable that the opposite should sometimes be the case. Some of the primitive presuppositions of human reason might have been correct and inevitable, whilst the tendency to deny them might have sprung from a plausible misunderstanding, or the exaggeration of a half-truth: so that the critical opinion itself, after destroying the spontaneous assumptions on which it rested, might be incapable of subsisting.

In Locke the central presuppositions, which he embraced heartily and without question, were those of common sense. He adopted what he calls a "plain, historical method", fit, in his own words, "to be brought into well-bred company and polite conversation". Men, "barely by the use of their natural faculties", might attain to all the knowledge possible or worth having. All children, he writes, "that are born into this world, being surrounded with bodies that perpetually and diversely affect them" have "a variety of ideas imprinted" on their minds. "External material things as objects of Sensation, and the operations of our own minds as objects of Reflection, are to me", he continues, "the only originals from which all our ideas take their beginnings." "Every act of sensation", he writes elsewhere, "when duly considered, gives us an equal view of both parts of nature, the corporeal and the spiritual. For whilst I know, by seeing or hearing, . . . that there is some corporeal being without me, the object of that sensation, I do more certainly know that there is some spiritual being within me that sees and hears."

Resting on these clear perceptions, the natural philosophy of Locke falls into two parts, one strictly physical and scientific, the other critical and psychological. In respect to the composition of matter, Locke accepted the most advanced theory of his day, which happened to be a very old one: the theory of Democritus that the material universe contains nothing but a multitude of solid atoms coursing through infinite space: but Locke added a religious note to this materialism by suggesting that infinite space, in its sublimity, must be an attribute of God. He also believed what few materialists would venture to assert, that if we could thoroughly examine the cosmic mechanism we should see the demonstrable necessity of every complication that ensues, even of the existence and character of mind: for it was no harder for God to endow matter with the power of thinking than to endow it with the power of moving.

In the atomic theory we have a graphic image asserted to describe accurately, or even exhaustively, the intrinsic constitution of things, or their primary qualities. Perhaps, in so far as physical hypotheses must remain graphic at all, it is an inevitable theory. It was first suggested by the wearing out and dissolution of all material objects, and by the specks of dust floating in a sunbeam; and it is confirmed, on an enlarged scale, by the stellar universe as conceived by modern astronomy. When today we talk of nuclei and electrons, if we imagine them at all, we imagine them as atoms. But it is all a picture, prophesying what we might see through a sufficiently powerful microscope; the important philosophical question is the one raised by the other half of Locke's natural philosophy, by optics and the general criticism of perception. How far, if at all, may we trust the images in our minds to reveal the nature of external things?

On this point the doctrine of Locke, through Descartes,[1] was also derived from Democritus. It was that all the sensible qualities of things, except position, shape, solidity, number and motion, were only ideas in us, projected and falsely regarded as lodged in things. In the things, these imputed or secondary qualities were simply powers, inherent in their atomic constitution, and calculated to excite sensations of that character in

[1] See note II, p. 29.

our bodies. This doctrine is readily established by Locke's plain historical method, when applied to the study of rainbows, mirrors, effects of perspective, dreams, jaundice, madness, and the will to believe: all of which go to convince us that the ideas which we impulsively assume to be qualities of objects are always, in their seat and origin, evolved in our own heads.

These two parts of Locke's natural philosophy, however, are not in perfect equilibrium. *All* the feelings and ideas of an animal must be equally conditioned by his organs and passions,[1] and he cannot be aware of what goes on beyond him, except as it affects his own life.[2] How then could Locke, or could Democritus, suppose that his ideas of space and atoms were less human, less graphic, summary, and symbolic, than his sensations of sound or colour? The language of science, no less than that of sense, should have been recognised to be a human language; and the nature of anything existent collateral with ourselves, be that collateral existence material or mental, should have been confessed to be a subject for faith and

[1] See note III, p. 35. [2] See note IV, p. 36.

for hypothesis, never, by any possibility, for absolute or direct intuition.

There is no occasion to take alarm at this doctrine as if it condemned us to solitary confinement, and to ignorance of the world in which we live. We see and know the world through our eyes and our intelligence, in visual and in intellectual terms: how else should a world be seen or known which is not the figment of a dream, but a collateral power, pressing and alien? In the cognisance which an animal may take of his surroundings—and surely all animals take such cognisance—the subjective and moral character of his feelings, on finding himself so surrounded, does not destroy their cognitive value. These feelings, as Locke says, are signs: to take them for signs is the essence of intelligence. Animals that are sensitive physically are also sensitive morally, and feel the friendliness or hostility which surrounds them. Even pain and pleasure are no idle sensations, satisfied with their own presence: they violently summon attention to the objects that are their source. Can love or hate be felt without being felt towards something—something near and potent, yet external, uncontrolled, and mysterious? When I dodge a missile or pick a berry, is it likely that my mind should stop to dwell on its pure sensations or ideas without recognising or pursuing something material? Analytic reflection often ignores the essential energy of mind, which is originally more intelligent than sensuous, more appetitive and dogmatic than aesthetic. But the feelings and ideas of an active animal cannot help uniting internal moral intensity with external physical reference; and the natural conditions of sensibility require that perceptions should owe their existence and quality to the living organism with its moral bias, and that at the same time they should be addressed to the external objects which entice that organism or threaten it.

All ambitions must be defeated when they ask for the impossible. The ambition to know is not an exception; and certainly our perceptions cannot tell us how the world would look if nobody saw it, or how valuable it would be if nobody cared for it. But our perceptions, as Locke again said, are sufficient for our welfare and appropriate to our condition. They are not only a wonderful entertainment in themselves, but apart from their sensuous and grammatical quality, by their distribution and method of variation, they may inform us most exactly about the order and mechanism of nature. We see in the science of today how completely the most accurate knowledge—proved to be accurate by its application in the arts—may shed every pictorial element, and the whole language of experience, to become a pure method of calculation and control. And by a pleasant compensation, our aesthetic life may become freer, more self-sufficing, more humbly happy in itself: and without trespassing in any way beyond the modesty of nature, we may consent to be like little children, chirping our human note; since the life of reason in us may well become science in its validity, whilst remaining poetry in its texture.

I think, then, that by a slight re-arrangement of Locke's pronouncements in natural philosophy, they could be made inwardly consistent, and still faithful to the first presuppositions of common sense, although certainly far more chastened and sceptical than impulsive opinion is likely to be in the first instance.

There were other presuppositions in the philosophy of Locke besides his fundamental naturalism; and in his private mind probably the most important was his Christian faith, which was not only confident and sincere, but prompted him at times to high speculation. He had friends among the Cambridge Platonists, and he found in Newton a brilliant example of scientific rigour capped with mystical insights. Yet if we consider Locke's philosophical position in the abstract, his Christianity almost disappears. In form his theology and ethics were strictly rationalistic; yet one who was a Deist in philosophy might remain a Christian in religion. There was no great harm in a special revelation, provided it were simple and short, and left the broad field of truth open in almost every direction to free and personal investigation. A free man and a good man would certainly never admit, as coming from God, any doctrine contrary to his private reason or political interest; and the moral precepts actually vouchsafed to us in the Gospels were most acceptable, seeing that they added a sublime eloquence to maxims which sound reason would have arrived at in any case.

Evidently common sense had nothing to fear from religious faith of this character; but the matter could not end there. Common sense is not more convinced of anything than of the difference between good and evil, advantage and disaster; and it cannot dispense with a moral interpretation of the universe. Socrates, who spoke initially for common sense, even thought the moral interpretation of existence the whole of philosophy. He would not have seen anything comic in the satire of Molière making his chorus of young doctors chant in unison that opium causes sleep because it has a dormitive virtue. The virtues or moral uses of things, according to Socrates, were the reason why the things had been created and were what they were; the admirable virtues of opium defined its perfection, and the perfection of a thing was the full manifestation of its deepest nature. Doubtless this moral interpretation of the universe had been overdone, and it had been a capital error in Socrates to make that interpretation exclusive and to substitute it for natural philosophy. Locke, who was himself a medical man, knew what a black cloak for ignorance and villainy Scholastic verbiage might be in that profession. He also knew, being an enthusiast for experimental science, that in order to control the movement of matter—which is to realise those virtues and perfections—it is better to trace the movement of matter materialistically; for it is in the act of manifesting its own powers, and not, as Socrates and the Scholastics fancied, by obeying a foreign magic, that matter sometimes assumes or restores the forms so precious in the healer's or the moralist's eyes. At the same time, the manner in which the moral world rests upon the natural, though divined, perhaps, by a few philosophers, has not been generally understood; and Locke, whose broad humanity could not exclude the moral interpretation of nature, was driven in the end to the view of Socrates. He seriously invoked the Scholastic maxim that nothing can produce that which it does not contain. For this reason the unconscious, after all, could never have given rise to consciousness.

Observation and experiment could not be allowed to decide this point: the moral interpretation of things, because more deeply rooted in human experience, must envelop the physical interpretation, and must have the last word.

It was characteristic of Locke's simplicity and intensity that he retained these insulated sympathies in various quarters. A further instance of his many-sidedness was his fidelity to pure intuition, his respect for the infallible revelation of ideal being, such as we have of sensible qualities or of mathematical relations. In dreams and in hallucinations appearances may deceive us, and the objects we think we see may not exist at all. Yet in suffering an illusion we must entertain an idea; and the manifest character of these ideas is that of which alone, Locke thinks, we can have certain "knowledge".

"These", he writes, "are two very different things and carefully to be distinguished: it being one thing to perceive and know the idea of white or black, and quite another to examine what kind of particles they must be, and how arranged...to make any object appear white or black." "A man infallibly knows, as soon as ever he has them in his mind, that the ideas he calls white and round are the very ideas they are, and that they are not other ideas which he calls red or square.... This... the mind... always perceives at first sight; and if ever there happen any doubt about it, it will always be found to be about the names and not the ideas themselves."

This sounds like high Platonic doctrine for a philosopher of the Left; but Locke's utilitarian temper very soon reasserted itself in this subject. Mathematical ideas were not only lucid but true: and he demanded this truth, which he called "reality", of all ideas worthy of consideration: mere ideas would be worthless. Very likely he forgot, in his philosophic puritanism, that fiction and music might have an intrinsic charm. Where the frontier of human wisdom should be drawn in this direction was clearly indicated, in Locke's day, by Spinoza, who says:

"If, in keeping non-existent things present to the imagination, the mind were at the same time aware that those things did not exist, surely it would regard this gift of imagination as a virtue in its own constitution, not as a vice: especially if such an imaginative faculty depended on nothing except the mind's own nature: that is to say, if this mental faculty of imagination were free".

But Locke had not so firm a hold on truth that he could afford to play with fancy; and as he pushed forward the claims of human jurisdiction rather too far in physics, by assuming the current science to be literally true, so, in the realm of imagination, he retrenched somewhat illiberally our legitimate possessions. Strange that as modern philosophy transfers the visible wealth of nature more and more to the mind, the mind should seem to lose courage and to become ashamed of its own fertility. The hard-pressed natural man will not indulge his imagination unless it poses for truth; and being half aware of this imposition, he is more troubled at the thought of being deceived than at the fact of being mechanised or being bored: and he would wish to escape imagination altogether. A good God, he murmurs, could not have made us poets against our will.

Against his will, however, Locke was drawn to enlarge the subjective sphere. The actual existence of mind was evident: you had only to notice the fact that you were thinking. Conscious mind, being thus known to exist directly and independently of the body, was a primary constituent of reality: it was a fact on its own account.[1] Common sense seemed to testify to this, not only when confronted with the "I think, therefore I am" of Descartes, but whenever a thought produced an action. Since mind and body interacted,[2] each must be as real as the other and, as it were, on the same plane of being. Locke, like a good Protestant, felt the right of the conscious inner man to assert himself: and when he looked into his own mind, he found nothing to define this mind except the ideas which occupied it. The existence which he was so sure of in himself was therefore the existence of his ideas.

Here, by an insensible shift in the meaning of the word "idea", a momentous revolution had taken place in psychology. Ideas had originally meant objective terms distinguished in thought —images, qualities, concepts, propositions. But now ideas began to mean living thoughts, moments or states of consciousness. They became atoms of mind, constituents of experience, very

[1] See note v, p. 37. [2] See note vi, p. 39.

much as material atoms were conceived to be constituents of natural objects. Sensations became the only objects of sensation, and ideas the only objects of ideas; so that the material world was rendered superfluous, and the only scientific problem was now to construct a universe in terms of analytic psychology. Locke himself did not go so far, and continued to assign physical causes and physical objects to some, at least, of his mental units; and indeed sensations and ideas could not very well have other than physical causes, the existence of which this new psychology was soon to deny: so that about the origin of its data it was afterwards compelled to preserve a discreet silence. But as to their combinations and reappearances, it was able to invoke the principle of association: a thread on which many shrewd observations may be strung, but which also, when pressed, appears to be nothing but a verbal mask for organic habits in matter.

The fact is that there are two sorts of unobjectionable psychology, neither of which describes a mechanism of disembodied mental states, such as the followers of Locke developed into modern idealism, to the confusion of common sense.[1] One unobjectionable sort of psychology is biological, and studies life from the outside. The other sort, relying on memory and dramatic imagination, reproduces life from the inside, and is literary. If the literary psychologist is a man of genius, by the clearness and range of his memory, by quickness of sympathy and power of suggestion, he may come very near to the truth of experience, as it has been or might be unrolled in a human being.[2] The ideas with which Locke operates are simply high lights picked out by attention in this nebulous continuum, and identified by names. Ideas, in the original ideal sense of the word, are indeed the only definite terms which attention can discriminate and rest upon; but the unity of these units is specious, not existential. If ideas were not logical or aesthetic essences but self-subsisting feelings, each knowing itself, they would be insulated for ever; no spirit could ever survey, recognise, or compare them; and mind would have disappeared in the analysis of mind.

These considerations might enable us, I think,

[1] See note VII, p. 43.   [2] See note VIII, p. 46.

to mark the just frontier of common sense even in this debatable land of psychology. All that is biological, observable, and documentary in psychology falls within the lines of physical science and offers no difficulty in principle. Nor need literary psychology form a dangerous salient in the circuit of nature. The dramatic poet or dramatic historian necessarily retains the presupposition of a material world, since beyond his personal memory (and even within it) he has nothing to stimulate and control his dramatic imagination save knowledge of the material circumstances in which people live, and of the material expression in action or words which they give to their feelings. His moral insight simply vivifies the scene that nature and the sciences of nature spread out before him: they tell him what has happened, and his heart tells him what has been felt. Only literature can describe experience for the excellent reason that the terms of experience are moral and literary from the beginning. Mind is incorrigibly poetical: not because it is not attentive to material facts and practical exigencies, but because, being intensely attentive to them, it turns them into pleasures and pains, and into many-coloured ideas. Yet at every turn there is a possibility and an occasion for transmuting this poetry into science, because ideas and emotions, being caused by material events, refer to these events, and record their order.

All philosophies are frail, in that they are products of the human mind, in which everything is essentially reactive, spontaneous, and volatile: but as in passion and in language, so in philosophy, there are certain comparatively steady and hereditary principles, forming a sort of orthodox reason, which is or which may become the current grammar of mankind. Of philosophers who are orthodox in this sense, only the earliest or the most powerful, an Aristotle or a Spinoza, need to be remembered, in that they stamp their language and temper upon human reason itself. The rest of the orthodox are justly lost in the crowd and relegated to the chorus. The frailty of heretical philosophers is more conspicuous and interesting: it makes up the *chronique scandaleuse* of the mind, or the history of philosophy. Locke belongs to both camps: he was restive in his orthodoxy and timid in his heresies; and like so many other initiators of revolutions, he would be dismayed at the result of his work. In intention Locke occupied an almost normal philosophic position, rendered precarious not by what was traditional in it, like the categories of substance and power, but rather by certain incidental errors—notably by admitting an experience independent of bodily life, yet compounded and evolving in a mechanical fashion. But I do not find in him a prickly nest of obsolete notions and contradictions from which, fledged at last, we have flown to our present enlightenment. In his person, in his temper, in his allegiances and hopes, he was the prototype of a race of philosophers native and dominant among people of English speech, if not in academic circles, at least in the national mind. If we make allowance for a greater personal subtlety, and for the diffidence and perplexity inevitable in the present moral anarchy of the world, we may find this same Lockian eclecticism and prudence in the late Lord Balfour: and I have myself had the advantage of being the pupil of a gifted successor and, in many ways, emulator, of Locke, I mean

William James. So great, at bottom, does their spiritual kinship seem to me to be, that I can hardly conceive Locke vividly without seeing him as a sort of William James of the seventeenth century. And who of you has not known some other spontaneous, inquisitive, unsettled genius, no less preoccupied with the marvellous intelligence of some Brazilian parrot, than with the sad obstinacy of some Bishop of Worcester? Here is eternal freshness of conviction and ardour for reform; great keenness of perception in spots, and in other spots lacunae and impulsive judgments; distrust of tradition, of words, of constructive argument; horror of vested interests and of their smooth defenders; a love of navigating alone and exploring for oneself even the coasts already well charted by others. Here is romanticism united with a scientific conscience and power of destructive analysis balanced by moral enthusiasm. Doubtless Locke might have dug his foundations deeper and integrated his faith better. His system was no metaphysical castle, no theological acropolis: rather a homely ancestral manor house built in several styles of architecture: a Tudor chapel, a

Palladian front toward the new geometrical garden, a Jacobean parlour for political consultation and learned disputes, and even—since we are almost in the eighteenth century—a Chinese cabinet full of curios. It was a habitable philosophy, and not too inharmonious. There was no greater incongruity in its parts than in the gentle variations of English weather or in the qualified moods and insights of a civilised mind. Impoverished as we are, morally and humanly, we can no longer live in such a rambling mansion. It has become a national monument. On the days when it is open we revisit it with admiration; and those chambers and garden walks re-echo to us the clear dogmas and savoury diction of the sage —omnivorous, artless, loquacious—whose dwelling it was.

SUPPLEMENTARY NOTES

I

Page 3. *This airy monster, this half-natural changeling.*

Monsters and changelings were pointed to by Locke with a certain controversial relish: they proved that nature was not compressed or compressible within Aristotelian genera and species, but was a free mechanism subject to indefinite change. Mechanism in physics is favourable to liberty in politics and morals: each creature has a right to be what it spontaneously is, and not what some previous classification alleges that it ought to have been. The Protestant and revolutionary independence of Locke's mind here gives us a foretaste of Darwin and even of Nietzsche. But Locke was moderate even in his radicalisms. A human nature totally fluid would of itself have proved anarchical; but in order to stem that natural anarchy it was fortunately possible to invoke the conditions of prosperity and happiness strictly laid down by the Creator. The improvidence and naughtiness of nature was called to book at every turn by the pleasures and pains divinely appended to things enjoined and to things forbidden, and ultimately by hell and by heaven. Yet if rewards and punishments were attached to human action and feeling in this perfectly external and arbitrary fashion, whilst the feelings and actions spontaneous in mankind counted for nothing in the rule of morals and of wisdom, we should be living under the most cruel and artificial of tyrannies; and it would not be long before the authority of such a code would be called in question and the reality of those arbitrary rewards and punishments would be denied, both for this world and for any other. In a truly rational morality moral sanctions would have to vary with the variation of species, each new race or individual or mode of feeling finding its natural joy in a new way of life. The monsters would not be monsters except to rustic prejudice, and the changelings would be simply experiments in creation. The glee of Locke in seeing nature elude scholastic conventions would then lose its savour, since those staid conventions themselves would have become obsolete. Nature would henceforth present nothing but pervasive metamorphosis, irresponsible and endless. To correct the weariness of such pure flux we might indeed invoke the idea of a progress or evolution towards something always higher and better; but this idea simply reinstates, under a temporal form, the dominance of a specific standard, to which nature is asked to conform. Genera and species might shift and glide into one another at will, but always in the authorised direction. If, on the contrary, transformation had no predetermined direction, we should be driven back, for a moral principle, to each of the particular types of life generated on the way: as in estimating the correctness or beauty of language we appeal to the speech and genius of each nation at each epoch, without imposing the grammar of one language or age upon another. It is only in so far as, in the midst of the flux, certain tropes become organised and recurrent, that any interests or beauties can be transmitted from moment to moment or from generation to generation. Physical integration is a prerequisite to moral integrity; and unless an individual or a species is sufficiently organised and determinate to aspire to a distinguishable form of life, eschewing all others, that individual or species can bear no significant name, can achieve no progress, and can approach no beauty or perfection.

Thus, so long as in a fluid world there is some measure of life and organisation, monsters and changelings will always remain possible physically and regrettable morally. Small deviations from the chosen type or the chosen direction of progress will continue to be called morbid and ugly, and great deviations or reversals will continue to be called monstrous. This is but the seamy side of that spontaneous predilection, grounded in our deepest nature, by which we recognise beauty and nobleness at first sight, with immense refreshment and perfect certitude.

II

Page 8. *Through Descartes*.

Very characteristic was the tireless polemic which Locke carried on against Descartes. The outraged plain facts had to be defended against sweeping and arbitrary theories. There were no innate ideas or maxims: children were not born murmuring that things equal to the same thing were equal to one another: and an urchin knew that pain was caused by the paternal slipper before he reflected philosophically that everything must have a cause. Again, extension was not the essence of matter, which must be solid as well, to be distinguishable from empty space. Finally, thinking was not the essence of the soul: a man, without dying, might lose consciousness: this often happened, or at least could not be prevented from happening by a definition framed by a French philosopher. These protests were evidently justified by common sense: yet they missed the speculative radicalism and depth of the Cartesian doctrines, which had struck the keynotes of all modern philosophy and science: for they assumed, for the first time in history, the transcendental point of view. No wonder that Locke could not do justice to this great novelty: Descartes himself did not do so, but ignored his subjective first principles in the development of his system; and it was not until adopted by Kant, or rather by Fichte, that the transcendental method showed its true colours. Even today philosophers fumble with it, patching soliloquy with physics and physics with soliloquy. Moreover, Locke's misunderstandings of Descartes were partly justified by the latter's verbal concessions to tradition and authority. A man who has a clear head, and like Descartes is rendered by his aristocratic pride both courteous and disdainful, may readily conform to usage in his language, and even in his personal sentiments, without taking either too seriously: he is not struggling to free his own mind, which is free already, nor very hopeful of freeing that of most people. The innate ideas were not explicit thoughts but categories employed unwittingly, as people in speaking conform to the grammar of the vernacular without being aware that they do so. As for extension being the essence of matter, since matter existed and was a substance, it would always have been more than its essence: a sort of ether the parts of which might move and might have different and calculable dynamic values. The gist of this definition of matter was to clear the decks for scientific calculation, by removing from nature the moral density and moral magic with which the Socratic philosophy had encumbered it. Science would be employed in describing the movements of bodies, leaving it for the senses and feelings to appreciate the cross-lights that might be generated in the process. Though not following the technique of Descartes, the physics of our own day realises his ideal, and traces in nature a mathematical dynamism, perfectly sufficient for exact prevision and mechanical art.

Similarly, in saying that the essence of the soul was to think, Descartes detached consciousness, or actual spirit, from the meshes of all unknown organic or invented mental mechanisms. It was an immense clarification and liberation in its proper dimension: but this pure consciousness was not a soul; it was not the animal psyche, or principle of organisation, life, and passion—a principle which, according to Descartes, was material. To have called such a material principle the soul would have shocked all Christian conceptions; but if Descartes had abstained from giving that consecrated name to mere consciousness, he need not have been wary of making the latter intermittent and evanescent, as it naturally is. He was driven to the conclusion that the soul can never stop thinking, by the desire to placate orthodox opinion, and his own Christian sentiments, at the expense of attributing to actual consciousness a substantial independence and a directive physical force which were incongruous with it: a force and independence perfectly congruous with the Platonic soul, which had been a mythological being, a supernatural spirit or daemon or incubus, incarnate in the natural world, and partly dominating it. The relations of such a soul to the particular body or bodies which it might weave for itself on earth, to the actions which it performed through such bodies, and to the current of its own thoughts, then became questions for theology, or for a moralistic theory of the universe. They were questions remote from the preoccupations of the modern mind; yet it was not possible either for Locke or for Descartes to clear their fresh conceptions altogether from those ancient dreams.

What views precisely did Locke oppose to these radical tendencies of Descartes?

In respect to the nature of matter, I have indicated

above the position of Locke: pictorially he accepted an ordinary atomism; scientifically, the physics of Newton.

On the other two points Locke's convictions were implicit rather than speculative: he resisted the Cartesian theories without much developing his own, as after all was natural in a critic engaged in proving that our natural faculties were not intended for speculation. All knowledge came from experience, and no man could know the savour of a pineapple without having tasted it. Yet this savour, according to Locke, did not reside at first in the pineapple, to be conveyed on contact to the palate and to the mind; but it was generated in the process of gustation; or perhaps we should rather say that it was generated in the mind on occasion of that process. At least, then, in respect to secondary qualities, and to all moral values, the terms of human knowledge were not drawn from the objects encountered in the world, but from an innate sensibility proper to the human body or mind. Experience—if this word meant the lifelong train of ideas which made a man's moral being—was not a source of knowledge but was knowledge (or illusion) itself, produced by organs endowed with a special native sensibility in contact with varying external stimuli. This conclusion would then not have contradicted, but exactly expressed, the doctrine of innate categories.

As to the soul, which might exist without thinking, Locke still called it an immaterial substance: not so immaterial, however, as not to be conveyed bodily with him in his coach from London to Oxford. Although, like Hobbes, Locke believed in the power of the English language to clarify the human intellect, he here ignored the advice of Hobbes to turn that befuddling Latin phrase into plain English. Substance meant body: immaterial meant bodiless: therefore immaterial substance meant bodiless body. True, substance had not really meant body for Aristotle or the Schoolmen; but who now knew or cared what anything had meant for them? Locke scornfully refused to consider what a substantial form may have signified; and in still maintaining that he had a soul, and calling it a spiritual substance, he was probably simply protesting that there was something living and watchful within his breast, the invisible moral agent in all his thoughts and actions. It was *he* that had them and did them; and this self of his was far from being reducible to a merely logical impersonal subject, an "I think" presupposed in all thought: for what would this "I think" have become when it was not thinking? On the other hand it mattered very little what the *substance* of a thinking being might be: God might even have endowed the body with the faculty of thinking, and of generating ideas on occasion of certain impacts. Yet a man was a man for all that: and Locke was satisfied that he knew, at least well enough for an honest Englishman, what he was. He was what he felt himself to be: and this inner man of his was not merely the living self, throbbing now in his heart; it was all his moral past, all that he remembered to have been. If, from moment to moment, the self was a spiritual energy astir within, in retrospect the living present seemed, as it were, to extend its tentacles and to communicate its subjectivity to his whole personal past. The limits of his personality were those of his memory, and his experience included everything that his living mind could appropriate and re-live. In a word, *he was his idea of himself*: and this insight opens a new chapter not only in his philosophy but in the history of human self-estimation. Mankind was henceforth invited not to think of itself as a tribe of natural beings, nor of souls, with a specific nature and fixed possibilities. Each man was a romantic personage or literary character: he was simply what he was thought to be, and might become anything that he could will to become. The way was opened for Napoleon on the one hand and for Fichte on the other.

III

Page 9. All *ideas must be equally conditioned*.

Even the mathematical ideas which seem so exactly to describe the dynamic order of nature are not repetitions of their natural counterpart: for mathematical form in nature is a web of diffuse relations enacted; in the mind it is a thought possessed, the logical synthesis of those deployed relations. To run in a circle is one thing; to conceive a circle is another. Our mind by its animal roots (which render it relevant to the realm of matter and cognitive) and by its spiritual actuality (which renders it original, synthetic, and emotional) is a language, from its beginnings; almost, we might say, a biological poetry; and the greater the intellectuality and poetic abstraction the greater the possible range. Yet we must not expect this scope of speculation in us to go with adequacy or exhaustiveness: on the contrary, mathematics and religion, each in its way so sure, leave most of the truth out.

IV

Page 9. *He cannot be aware of what goes on beyond him, except as it affects his own life.*

Even that spark of divine intelligence which comes into the animal soul, as Aristotle says, from beyond the gates, comes and is called down by the exigencies of physical life. An animal endowed with locomotion cannot merely feast sensuously on things as they appear, but must react upon them at the first signal, and in so doing must virtually and in intent envisage them as they are in themselves. For it is by virtue of their real constitution and intrinsic energy that they act upon us and suffer change in turn at our hands; so that whatsoever form things may take to our senses and intellect, they take that form by exerting their material powers upon us, and intertwining them in action with our own organisms.

Thus the appearance of things is always, in some measure, a true index to their reality. Animals are inevitably engaged in self-transcending action, and the consciousness of self-transcending action is self-transcendent knowledge. The very nature of animal life makes it possible, within animal consciousness, to discount appearance and to correct illusion—things which in a vegetative or aesthetic sensibility would not be distinguishable from pure experience itself. But when aroused to self-transcendent attention, feeling must needs rise to intelligence, so that external fact and impartial truth come within the range of consciousness, not indeed by being contained there, but by being aimed at.

v

Page 19. *Conscious mind was a fact on its own account.*

This conscious mind was a man's moral being, and personal identity could not extend further than possible memory. This doctrine of Locke's had some comic applications. The Bishop of Worcester was alarmed. If actions which a hardened sinner had forgotten were no longer his, a short memory would be a great blessing in the Day of Judgment. On the other hand, a theology more plastic than Stillingfleet's would one day find in this same doctrine a new means of edification. For if I may disown all actions I have forgotten, may not things not done or witnessed by me in the body be now appropriated and incorporated in my consciousness, if only I conceive them vividly? The door is then open to all the noble ambiguities of idealism. As my consciousness expands, or thinks it expands, into dramatic sympathy with universal experience, that experience becomes my own. I may say I have been the agent in all past achievements. Emerson could know that he was Shakespeare and Caesar and Christ. Futurity is mine also, in every possible direction at once; and I am one with the spirit of the universe and with God.

Locke reassured the Bishop of Worcester, and was humbly confident that Divine Justice would find a way of vindicating Itself in spite of human wit. He might have added that if the sin of Adam could not only be imputed to us juridically but could actually taint our consciousness—as it certainly does if by Adam we understand our whole material heritage—so surely the sins done or the habits acquired by the body beyond the scope of consciousness may taint or clarify this consciousness now. Indeed, the idea we form of ourselves and of our respective experiences is a figment of vanity, a product of dramatic imagination, without cognitive import save as a reading of the hidden forces, physical or divine, which have formed us and actually govern us.

VI

Page 19. *Mind and body interacted.*

The self which acts in a man is itself moved by forces which have long been familiar to common sense, without being understood except dramatically. These forces are called the passions; or when the dramatic units distinguished are longish strands rather than striking episodes, they are called temperament, character, or will; or perhaps, weaving all these strands and episodes together again into one moral fabric, we call them simply human nature. But in what does this vague human nature reside, and how does it operate on the non-human world? Certainly not within the conscious sphere, or in the superficial miscellany of experience. Immediate experience is the intermittent chaos which human nature, in combination with external circumstances, is invoked to support and to rationalise. Is human nature, then, resident in each individual soul? Certainly: but the soul is merely another name for that active principle which we are looking for, to be the seat of our sensibility and the source of our actions. Is this psychic power, then, resident in the body? Undoubtedly; since it is hereditary and transmitted by a seed, and continually aroused and modified by material agencies.

Since this soul or self in the body is so obscure, the temptation is great to dramatise its energies and to describe them in myths. Myth is the normal means of describing those forces of nature which we cannot measure or understand; if we could understand or measure them we should describe them prosaically and analytically, in what is called science. But nothing is less measurable, or less intelligible to us, in spite of being so near us and familiar, as the life of this carnal instrument, so soft and so violent, which breeds our sensations and precipitates our actions. We see today how the Freudian psychology, just because it is not satisfied with registering the routine of consciousness but endeavours to trace its hidden mechanism and to unravel its physical causes, is driven to use the most frankly mythological language. The physiological processes concerned, though presupposed, are not on the scale of human perception and not traceable in detail; and the moral action, though familiar in snatches, has to be patched by invented episodes, and largely attributed to daemonic personages that never come on the stage.

Locke, in his psychology of morals, had at first followed the verbal rationalism by which people attribute motives to themselves and to one another.

Human actions were explained by the alleged pursuit of the greater prospective pleasure, and avoidance of the greater prospective pain. But this way of talking, though not so poetical as Freud's, is no less mythical. Eventual goods and evils have no present existence and no power: they cannot even be discerned prophetically, save by the vaguest fancy, entirely based on the present impulses and obsessions of the soul. No future good, no future evil avails to move us, except—as Locke said after examining the facts more closely—when *a certain uneasiness* in the soul (or in the body) causes us to turn to those untried goods and evils with a present and living interest. This actual uneasiness, with the dream pictures which it evokes, is a mere symptom of the direction in which human nature in us is already moving, or already disposed to move. Without this prior physical impulse, heaven may beckon and hell may yawn without causing the least variation in conduct. As in religious conversion all is due to the call of grace, so in ordinary action all is due to the ripening of natural impulses and powers within the psyche. The *uneasiness* observed by Locke is merely the consciousness of this ripening, before the field of relevant action has been clearly discerned.

When all this is considered, the ostensible interaction between mind and body puts on a new aspect. There are no *purely mental* ideas or intentions followed by material effects: there are no material events followed by a *purely mental* sensation or idea. Mental events are always elements in total natural events containing material elements also: material elements form the organ, the stimulus, and probably also the object for those mental sensations or ideas. Moreover, the physical strand alone is found to be continuous and traceable; the conscious strand, the sequence of mental events, flares up and dies down daily, if not hourly; and the medley of its immediate features—images, words, moods—juxtaposes China and Peru, past and future, in the most irresponsible confusion. On the other hand, in human life it is a part of the conscious element—intentions, affections, plans, and reasonings—that *explains* the course of action: dispersed temporally, our dominant thoughts contain the reason for our continuous behaviour, and seem to guide it. They are not so much links in a chain of minute consecutive causes—an idea or an act of will often takes time to work and works, as it were, only posthumously—as they are general over-arching moral inspirations and resolves, which the machinery of our bodies executes in its own way, often rendering our thoughts more precise in the process, or totally transforming them. We do roughly what we meant to do, barring accidents. The reasons lie deep in our compound nature, being probably inarticulate; and our action in a fragmentary way betrays our moral disposition: betrays it in both senses of the word betray, now revealing it unawares, and now sadly disappointing it.

I leave it for the reader's reflection to decide whether we should call such cohabitation of mind with body interaction, or not rather sympathetic concomitance, self-annotation, and a partial prophetic awakening to a life which we are leading automatically.

VII

Page 21. *To the confusion of common sense.*

Berkeley and his followers sometimes maintain that common sense is on their side, that they have simply analysed the fact of our experience of the material world, and if there is any paradox in their idealism, it is merely verbal and disappears with familiarity. All the "reality", they say, all the force, obduracy, and fertility of nature subsist undiminished after we discover that this reality resides, and can only reside, in the fixed order of our experience.

But no: analysis of immediate experience will never disclose any fixed order in it; the surface of experience, when not interpreted materialistically, is an inextricable dream. Berkeley and his followers, when they look in this direction, towards nature and the rationale of experience and science, are looking away from their own system, and relying instead on the automatic propensity of human nature to routine, so that we spontaneously prepare for repeating our actions (not our experience) and even anticipate their occasions; a propensity further biased by the dominant rhythms of the psyche, so that we assume a future not so much similar to the past, as better. When developed, this propensity turns into trust in natural or divine laws; but it is contrary to common sense to expect such laws to operate apart from matter and from the material continuity of external occasions. This appears clearly in our trust in persons —a radical animal propensity—which is consonant with common sense when these persons are living bodies, but becomes superstitious, or at least highly speculative, when these persons are disembodied spirits.

It is a pity that the beautiful system of Berkeley should have appeared in an unspiritual age, when religion was mundane and perfunctory, and the free spirit, where it stirred, was romantic and wilful. For that system was essentially religious: it put the spirit face to face with God, everywhere, always, and in everything; it turned experience into a divine language for the monition and expression of the inner man. Such an instrument, in spiritual hands, might have served to dispel all natural illusions and affections, and to disinfect the spirit of worldliness and egotism. But Berkeley and his followers had no such thought. All they wished was to substitute a social for a material world, precisely because a merely social world might make worldly interests loom

COMMON SENSE

larger and might induce mankind, against the evidence of their senses and the still small voice in their hearts, to live as if their worldly interests were absolute and must needs dominate the spirit.

Morally this system thus came to sanction a human servitude to material things such as ancient materialists would have scorned; and theoretically the system did not escape the dogmatic commitments of common sense against which it protested. For far from withdrawing into the depths of the private spirit, it professed to describe universal experience and the evolution of all human ideas. This notion of "experience" originally presupposed a natural agent or subject to endure that experience, and to profit by it, by learning to live in better harmony with external circumstances. Each agent or subject of experience might, at other times, become an object of experience also: for they all formed part of a material world, which they might envisage in common in their perceptions. Now the criticism which repudiates this common material medium, like all criticism or doubt, is secondary and partial: it continues to operate with all the assumptions of common sense, save the one which it is expressly criticising. So, in repudiating the material world, this philosophy retains the notion of various agents or subjects gathering experience; and we are not expected to doubt that there are just as many streams of experience without a world, as there were people in the world when the world existed. But the number and nature of these experiences have now become undiscoverable, the material persons having been removed who formerly were so placed as to gather easily imagined experiences, and to be able to communicate them; and the very notion of experience has been emptied of its meaning, when no external common world subsists to impose that same experience on everybody. It was not knowledge of existing experiences *in vacuo* that led common sense to assume a material world, but knowledge of an existing material world led it to assume existing, and regularly reproducible, experiences.

Thus the whole social convention posited by empirical idealism is borrowed without leave, and rests on the belief in nature for which it is substituted.

VIII

Page 21. *The literary psychologist may come very near to the truth of experience.*

Experience cannot be in itself an object of science, because it is essentially invisible, immeasurable, fugitive, and private; and although it may be shared or repeated, the evidence for that repetition or that unanimity cannot be found by comparing a present experience with another experience by hypothesis absent. Both the absent experience and its agreement with the present experience must be imagined freely and credited instinctively, in view of the known circumstances in which the absent experience is conceived to have occurred. The only instrument for conceiving experience at large is accordingly private imagination; and such imagination cannot be tested, although it may be guided and perhaps recast by fresh observations or reports concerning the action and language of other people. For action and language, being contagious, and being the material counterpart of experience in each of us, may voluntarily or involuntarily suggest our respective experience to one another, by causing each to re-enact more or less accurately within himself the experience of the rest. Thus alien thoughts and feelings are revealed or suggested to us in common life, not without a subjective transformation increasing, so to speak, as the square of the distance: and even the record of experience in people's own words, when these are not names for recognisable external things, awakens in the reader, in another age or country, quite incommensurable ideas. Yet, under favourable circumstances, such suggestion or revelation of experience, without ever becoming science, may become public unanimity in sentiment, and may produce a truthful and lively dramatic literature.

All modern philosophy, in so far as it is a description of experience and not of nature, therefore seems to belong to the sphere of literature, and to be without scientific value.

II

FIFTY YEARS OF BRITISH IDEALISM[1]

AFTER fifty years, an old milestone in the path of philosophy, Bradley's *Ethical Studies*, has been set up again, as if to mark the distance which English opinion has traversed in the interval. It has passed from insular dogmatism to universal bewilderment; and a chief agent in the change has been Bradley himself, with his scornful and delicate intellect, his wit, his candour, his persistence, and the baffling futility of his conclusions. In this early book we see him coming forth like a young David against every clumsy champion of utilitarianism, hedonism, positivism, or empiricism. And how smooth and polished were the little stones in his sling! How fatally they would have lodged in the forehead of that composite monster, if only it

[1] *Ethical Studies*, by F. H. Bradley, O.M., LL.D. (Glasgow), late Fellow of Merton College, Oxford; second edition revised, with additional notes by the Author. Oxford, The Clarendon Press, 1927.

had had a forehead! Some of them might even have done murderous execution in Bradley's own camp: for instance, this pebble cast playfully at the metaphysical idol called "Law": "It is *always* wet on half-holidays because of the Law of Raininess, but *sometimes* it is *not* wet, because of the Supplementary Law of Sunshine".

Bradley and his friends achieved a notable victory in the academic field: philosophic authority and influence passed largely into their hands in all English-speaking universities. But it was not exactly from these seats of learning that naturalism and utilitarianism needed to be dislodged; like the corresponding radicalisms of our day, these doctrines prevailed rather in certain political and intellectual circles outside, consciously revolutionary and often half-educated; and I am afraid that the braggart Goliaths of today need chastening at least as much as those of fifty years ago. In a country officially Christian, and especially in Oxford, it is natural and fitting that academic authority should belong to orthodox tradition—theological, Platonic, and Aristotelian. Bradley, save for a few learned quotations, strangely ignored this orthodoxy entrenched behind his back. In contrast with it he was himself a heretic, with first principles devastating every settled belief: and it was really this venerable silent partner at home that his victory superseded, at least in appearance and for a season. David did not slay Goliath, but he dethroned Saul. Saul was indeed already under a cloud, and all in David's heart was not unkindness in that direction. Bradley might almost be called an unbelieving Newman; time, especially, seems to have brought his suffering and refined spirit into greater sympathy with ancient sanctities. Originally, for instance, venting the hearty Protestant sentiment that only the Christianity of laymen is sound, he had written: "I am happy to say that 'religieux' has no English equivalent". But a later note says: "This is not true except of Modern English only. And, in any case, it won't do, and was wrong and due to ignorance. However secluded the religious life, it may be practical indirectly *if* through the unity of the spiritual body it can be taken as vicarious". The "*if*" here saves the principle that all values must be social, and that the social organism is the sole moral reality: yet how near this bubble comes to being pricked! We seem clearly to feel that the question is not whether spiritual life subserves animal society, but whether animal society ever is stirred and hallowed into spiritual life.

All this, however, in that age of progress, was regarded as obsolete: there was no longer to be any spirit except the spirit of the times. True, the ritualists might be striving to revive the latent energies of religious devotion, with some dubious help from aestheticism: but against the rising tide of mechanical progress and romantic anarchy, and against the mania for rewriting history, traditional philosophy then seemed helpless and afraid to defend itself: it is only now beginning to recover its intellectual courage. For the moment, speculative radicals saw light in a different quarter. German idealism was nothing if not self-confident; it was relatively new; it was encyclopaedic in its display of knowledge, which it could manipulate dialectically with dazzling, if not stable, results; it was Protestant in temper and autonomous in principle; and altogether it seemed a sovereign and providential means of suddenly turning the tables on the threatened naturalism. By developing romantic intuition from within and packing all knowledge into one picture, the universe might be shown to be, like intuition itself, thoroughly spiritual, personal, and subjective.

The fundamental axiom of the new logic was that the only possible reality was consciousness.

"People find", writes Bradley, "a subject and an object correlated in consciousness.... To go out of that unity is for us literally to go out of our minds.... When mind is made only a part of the whole, there is a question which *must* be answered.... If about any matter we know nothing whatsoever, can we say anything about it? Can we even say that it is? And if it is not in consciousness, how can we know it?... And conversely, if we know it, it cannot be not mind."

Bradley challenged his contemporaries to refute this argument; and not being able to do so, many of them felt constrained to accept it, perhaps not without grave misgivings. For was it not always a rooted conviction of the British mind that knowledge brings material power, and that any figments of consciousness (in religion, for instance) not bringing material power are dangerous bewitchments, and not properly knowledge? Yet it is no less characteristic of the British mind to yield occasionally, up to a certain point, to some such enthusiastic fancy, provided that its incompatibility with honest action may be denied or ignored. So in this case British idealists, in the act of defining knowledge idealistically, as the presence to consciousness of its own phenomena, never really ceased to assume transcendent knowledge of a self-existing world, social and psychological, if not material: and they continued scrupulously to readjust their ideas to those dark facts, often more faithfully than the avowed positivists or scientific psychologists.

What could ethics properly be to a philosopher who on principle might not trespass beyond the limits of consciousness? Only ethical sentiment. Bradley was satisfied to appeal to the moral consciousness of his day, without seeking to transform it. The most intentionally eloquent passage in his book describes war-fever unifying and carrying away a whole people: that was the summit of moral consciousness and of mystic virtue. His aim, even in ethics, was avowedly to describe that which exists, to describe moral experience, without proposing a different form for it. A man must be a man of his own time, or nothing; to set up to be better than the world was the beginning of immorality; and virtue lay in accepting one's station and its duties. The moralist should fill his mind with a concrete picture of the task and standards of his age and nation, and should graft his own ideals upon that tree; this need not prevent moral consciousness from including a decided esteem for non-political excellences like health, beauty, or intelligence, which are not ordinarily called virtues by modern moralists. Yet they were undeniably good; better, perhaps, than any painful and laborious dutifulness; so that the strictly moral consciousness might run over, and presently lose itself in "something higher". Indeed, even health, beauty, and intelligence, which seemed at first so clearly good, might lose their sharpness on a wider view. In the panorama that would ultimately fill the mind these so-called goods and virtues could not be conceived without their complementary vices and evils. Thus all moral consciousness, and even all vital preference might ultimately be superseded: they might appear to have belonged to a partial and rather low stage in the self-development of consciousness.

With this dissolution of his moral judgments always in prospect, why should Bradley, or any idealist, have pursued ethical studies at all? Since all phases of life were equally necessary to enrich an infinite consciousness, which must know both good and evil in order to merge and to transcend them, he could hardly nurse any intense enthusiasm for a different complexion to be given to the lives of men. His moral passion—for he had it, caustic and burning clear—was purely intellectual: it was shame that in England the moral consciousness should have been expressed in systems dialectically so primitive as those of the positivists and utilitarians. He acknowledged, somewhat superciliously, that their hearts were in the right place; yet, if we are to have ethics at all, were not their thoughts in the right place also? They were concerned not with analysis of the moral consciousness but with the conduct of affairs and the reform of institutions. The spectacle of human wretchedness profoundly moved them; their minds were bent on transforming society, so that a man's station and its duties might cease to be what a decayed feudal organisation and an inhuman industrialism had made of them. They revolted against the miserable condition of the masses of mankind, and against the miserable consolations which official religion, or a philosophy like Bradley's, offered them in their misery. The utilitarians were at least intent on existence and on the course of events; they wished to transform institutions to fit human nature better, and to educate human nature by those new institutions so that it might better realise its latent capacities. These are matters which a man may modify by his acts and they are therefore the proper concern of the moralist. Were they much to blame if they neglected to define pleasure or happiness and used catch-words, dialectically vague, to indicate a direction of effort politically quite unmistakable? Doubtless their political action, like their philosophical nomenclature, was revolutionary and relied too much on wayward feelings ignorant of their own causes. Revolution, no less than tradition, is but a casual and clumsy expression of human nature in contact with circumstances; yet pain and pleasure and spontaneous hopes, however foolish, are direct expressions of that contact, and speak for the soul; whereas a man's station and its duties are purely conventional, and may altogether misrepresent his native capacities. The protest of human nature against the world and its oppressions is the strong side of every rebellion; it was the *moral* side of utilitarianism, of the rebellion against irrational morality.

Unfortunately the English reformers were themselves idealists of a sort, entangled in the vehicles of perception, and talking about sensations and ideas, pleasures and pains, as if these had been the elements of human nature, or even of nature at large: and only the most meagre of verbal systems, and the most artificial, can be constructed out of such materials. Moreover, they spoke much of pleasure and happiness, and hardly at all of misery and pain: whereas it would have been wiser, and truer to their real inspiration, to have laid all the emphasis on evils to be abated, leaving the good to shape itself in freedom. Suffering is the instant and obvious sign of some outrage done to human nature; without this natural recoil, actual or imminent, no morality would have any sanction, and no precept could be imperative. What silliness to command me to pursue pleasure or to avoid it, if in any case everything would be well! Save for some shadow of dire repentance looming in the distance, I am deeply free to walk as I will. The choice of pleasure for a principle of morals was particularly unfortunate in the British utilitarians; it lent them an air of frivolity absurdly contrary to their true character. Pleasure might have been a fit enough word in the mouth of Aristippus, a semi-oriental untouched by the least sense of responsibility, or even on the lips of humanists in the eighteenth century, who, however sordid their lives may sometimes have been, could still move in imagination to the music of Mozart, in the landscape of Watteau or of Fragonard. But in the land and age of Dickens the moral ideal was not so much pleasure as kindness: this tenderer word not only expresses better the motive at work, but it points to the distressing presence of misery in the world, to make natural kindness laborious and earnest, and turn it into a legislative system.

Bradley's hostility to pleasure was not fanatical: one's station and its duties might have their agreeable side. "It is probably good for you", he tells us, "to have, say, not less than two glasses of wine after dinner. Six on ordinary occasions is perhaps too many; but as to three or four, they are neither one way nor the other." If the voluptuary was condemned, it was for the commonplace reason which a hedonist, too, might invoke, that a life of pleasure soon palls and becomes unpleasant. Bradley's objection to pleasure was merely speculative: he found it too "abstract". To call a pleasure when actually felt an abstraction is an exquisite absurdity: but pleasure, in its absolute essence, is certainly simple and indefinable. If instead of enjoying it on the wing, and as an earnest of the soul's momentary harmony, we attempt to arrest and observe it, we find it strangely dumb; we are not informed by it concerning its occasion, nor carried from it by any logical implication to the natural object in which it might be found. A pure hedonist ought therefore to be rather relieved if all images lapsed from his consciousness and he could luxuriate in sheer pleasure, dark and overwhelming. True, such bliss would be rather inhuman, and of the sort which we rashly assign to the oyster: but why should a radical and intrepid philosopher be ashamed of that? The condition of Bradley's Absolute—feeling in which all distinctions are transcended and merged—seems to be something of that kind; but there would be a strange irony in attributing this mystical and rapturous ideal to such ponderous worthies as Mill and Spencer, whose minds were nothing if not anxious, perturbed, instrumental, and full of respect for variegated facts, and who were probably incapable of tasting pure pleasure at all.

But if pleasure, in its pure essence, might really be the highest good for a mystic who should be lost in it, it would be no guide to a moralist wishing to control events, and to distribute particular pleasures or series of pleasures as richly as possible in the world. For this purpose he would need to understand human nature and its variable functions, in which different persons and peoples may find their sincere pleasures; and this knowledge would first lend to his general love of pleasure any point of application in the governance of life or in benevolent legislation. Some concrete image of a happy human world would take the place of the futile truism that pleasure is good and pain evil. This is, of course, what utilitarian moralists meant to do, and actually did, in so far as their human sympathies extended, which was not to the highest things; but it was not what they said, and Bradley had a clear advantage over them in the war of words. A pleasure is not a programme: it exists here and not there, for me and for no one else, once and never again. When past, it leaves the will as empty and as devoid of allegiance as if it had never existed; pleasure is sand, though it have the colour of gold. But this is evidently true of all existence. Each living moment, each dead man, each cycle of the universe leaves nothing behind it but a void which perhaps something kindred may refill. A Hegel, after identifying himself for a moment with the Absolute Idea, is in his existence no less subject to sleepiness, irritation, and death than if he had been modestly satisfied with the joys of an oyster. It is only their common form, or their common worship, that can give to the quick moments of life any mutual relevance or sympathy; and existence would not come at all within sight of a good, either momentary or final, if it were not inwardly directed upon realising some definite essence. For the rest this essence may be as simple as you will, if the nature directed upon it is unified and simple; and it would be mere intellectual snobbery to condemn pleasure because it has not so many subdivisions in it as an encyclopaedia of the sciences. For the moralist pleasure and pain may even be the better guides, because they express more directly and boldly the instinctive direction of animal life, and thereby mark more clearly the genuine difference between good and evil.

We may well say with Bradley that the good is self-realisation; but what is the self? Certainly not the feeling or consciousness of the moment, nor the life of the world, nor pure spirit. The self that can systematically distinguish good from evil is an animal soul. It grows from a seed; its potentiality is definite and its fate precarious; and in man it requires society to rear it and tradition to educate it. The good is accordingly social, in so far as the soul demands society; but it is the nature of the individual that determines the kind and degree of sociability that is good for him, and draws the line between society that is a benefit and society that is a nuisance. To subordinate the soul fundamentally to society or the individual to the state is sheer barbarism: the Greeks, sometimes invoked to support this form of idolatry, were never guilty of it; on the contrary, their lawgivers were always reforming and planning the state so that the soul might be perfect in it. Discipline is a help to the spirit: but even social relations, when like love, friendship, or sport they are spontaneous and good in themselves, retire as far as possible from the pressure of the world, and build their paradise apart, simple, and hidden in the wilderness; while all the ultimate hopes and assurances of the spirit escape altogether into the silent society of nature, of truth, of essence, far from those fatuous worldly conventions which hardly make up for their tyranny by their instability: for the prevalent moral fashion is always growing old, and human nature is always becoming young again. World-worship is the expedient of those who, having lost the soul that is in them, look for it in things external, where there is no soul: and by a curious recoil, it is also the expedient of those who seek their lost soul in actual consciousness, where it also is not: for sensations and ideas are not the soul but only passing and partial products of its profound animal life. Moral consciousness in particular would never have arisen and would be gratuitous, save for the ferocious bias of a natural living creature, defending itself against its thousand enemies.

Nor would knowledge in its turn be knowledge if it were merely intuition of essence, such as the sensualist, the poet, or the dialectician may rest in. If the imagery of logic or passion ever comes to convey *knowledge*, it does so by virtue of a concomitant physical adjustment to external things; for the nerve of real or transcendent knowledge is the notice which one part of the world may take of another part; and it is this momentous cognisance, no matter what intangible feelings may supply terms for its prosody, that enlarges the mind to some practical purpose and informs it about the world. Consciousness then ceases to be passive sense or idle ideation and becomes belief and intelligence. Then the essences which form the "content of consciousness" may be vivified and trippingly run over, like the syllables of a familiar word, in the active recognition of things and people and of all the ominous or pliable forces of nature. For essences, being eternal and non-existent in themselves, cannot come to consciousness by their own initiative, but only as occasion and the subtle movements of the soul may evoke their forms; so that the fact that they are given to consciousness has a natural status and setting in the material world, and is part of the same natural event as the movement of the soul and body which supports that consciousness.

There is therefore no need of refuting idealism, which is an honest examination of conscience in a reflective mind. Refutations and proofs depend on pregnant meanings assigned to terms, meanings first rendered explicit and unambiguous by those very proofs or refutations. On any different acceptation of those terms, these proofs and refutations fall to the ground; and it remains a question for good sense, not for logic at all, how far the terms in either case describe anything existent. If by "knowledge" we understand intuition of essences, idealism follows; but it follows only in respect to essences given in intuition: nothing follows concerning the seat, origin, conditions, or symptomatic value of such intuition, nor even that such intuition ever actually occurs. Idealism, therefore, without being refuted, may be hemmed in and humanised by natural knowledge about it and about its place in human speculation; the most recalcitrant materialist (like myself) might see its plausibility during a somewhat adolescent phase of self-consciousness. Consciousness itself he might accept and relish as the natural spiritual resonance of action and passion, recognising it in its proud isolation and specious autonomy, like the mountain republics of Andorra and San Marino.

German idealism is a mighty pose, an attitude always possible to a self-conscious and reflective being: but it is hardly a system, since it contradicts beliefs which in action are inevitable; it may therefore be readily swallowed, but it can never be digested. Neither of its two ingredients—romantic scepticism and romantic superstition—agrees particularly with the British stomach. Not romantic scepticism: for in England an instinctive distrust of too much clearness and logic, a difficulty in drawing all the consequences of any principle, soon gave to this most radical of philosophies a prim and religious air: its purity was alloyed with all sorts of conventions: so much so that we find British Hegelians often deeply engaged in psychology, cosmology, or religion, as if they took their idealism for a kind of physics, and wished merely to reinterpret the facts of nature in an edifying way, without uprooting them from their natural places. This has been made easier by giving idealism an objective, non-psychological turn: events, and especially feelings and ideas, will then be swallowed up in the essences which they display. Thus Bradley maintained that two thoughts, no matter how remote from each other in time or space, were identically the same, and not merely similar, if only they contemplated the same idea. Mind itself ceased in this way to mean a series of existing feelings and was identified with intelligence; and intelligence in its turn was identified with the Idea or Logos which might be the ultimate theme of intelligence. There could be only one mind, so conceived, since there could be only one total system in the universe visible to omniscience.

As to romantic scepticism, we may see by contrast what it would be, when left to itself, if we consider those lucid Italians who have taken up their idealism late and with open eyes. In Croce and Gentile the transcendental attitude is kept pure: for them there is really no universe save spirit creating its experience; and if we ask whence or on what principle occasions arise for all this compulsory fiction, we are reminded that this question, with any answer which spirit might invent for it, belongs not to philosophy but to some special science like physiology, itself, of course, only a particular product of creative thought. Thus the more impetuously the inquisitive squirrel would rush from his cage, the faster and faster he causes the cage to whirl about his ears. He has not the remotest chance of reaching his imaginary bait—God, nature, or truth; for to seek such things is to presuppose them, and to presuppose anything, if spirit be absolute, is to invent it. Even those philosophies of history which the idealist may for some secret reason be impelled to construct would be superstitious, according to his own principles, if he took them for more than poetic fictions of the historian; so that in the study of history, as in every other study, all the diligence and sober learning which the philosopher may possess are non-philosophical, since they presuppose independent events and material documents. Thus perfect idealism turns out to be pure literary sport, like lyric poetry, in which no truth is conveyed save the miscellaneous truths taken over from common sense or the special sciences; and the gay spirit, supposed to be living and shining of its own sweet will, can find nothing to live or shine upon save the common natural world.

Such at least would be the case if romantic superstition did not supervene, demanding that the spirit should impose some arbitrary rhythm or destiny on the world which it creates: but this side of idealism has been cultivated chiefly by the intrepid Germans: some of them, like Spengler and Keyserling, still thrive and grow famous on it without a blush. The modest English in these matters take shelter under the wing of science speculatively extended, or traditional religion prudently rationalised: the scope of the spirit, like its psychological distribution, is conceived realistically. It might almost prove an euthanasia for British idealism to lose itself in the new metaphysics of nature which the mathematicians are evolving; and since this metaphysics, though materialistic in effect, is more subtle and abstruse than popular materialism, British idealism might perhaps be said to survive in it, having now passed victoriously into its opposite, and being merged in something higher.

III

REVOLUTIONS IN SCIENCE

SINCE the beginning of the twentieth century, science has gained notably in expertness, and lost notably in authority. We are bombarded with inventions; but if we ask the inventors what they have learned of the depths of nature, which somehow they have probed with such astonishing success, their faces remain blank. They may be chewing gum; or they may tell us that if an aeroplane could only fly fast enough, it would get home before it starts; or they may urge us to come with them into a dark room, to hold hands, and to commune with the dear departed.

Practically there may be no harm in such a division of labour, the inventors doing the work and the professors the talking. The experts may themselves be inexpert in verbal expression, or content with stock phrases, or profoundly sceptical, or too busy to think. Nevertheless, skill and understanding are at their best when they go together and adorn the same mind. Modern science until lately had realised this ideal: it was an extension of common perception and common sense. We could trust it implicitly, as we do a map or a calendar; it was not true for us merely in an argumentative or visionary sense, as are religion and philosophy. Geography went hand in hand with travel, Copernican astronomy with circumnavigation of the globe: and even the theory of evolution and the historical sciences in the nineteenth century were continuous with liberal reform: people saw in the past, as they then learned to conceive it, simply an extension of those transformations which they were witnessing in the present. They could think they knew the world as a man knows his native town, or the contents of his chest of drawers: nature was our home, and science was our home knowledge. For it is not intrinsic clearness or coherence that make ideas persuasive, but connection with action, or with some voluminous inner response, which is readiness to act. It is a sense of on-coming fate, a compulsion to do or to suffer, that produces the illusion of perfect knowledge.

I call it illusion, although our contact with things may be real, and our sensations and thoughts may be inevitable and honest; because nevertheless it is always an illusion to suppose that our images are the intrinsic qualities of things, or reproduce them exactly. The Ptolemaic system, for instance, was perfectly scientific; it was based on careful and prolonged observation and on just reasoning; but it was modelled on an image—the spherical blue dome of the heavens—proper only to an observer on the earth, and not transferable to a universe which is diffuse, centreless, fluid, and perhaps infinite. When the imagination, for any reason, comes to be peopled with images of the latter sort, the modern, and especially the latest, astronomy becomes more persuasive. For although I suspect that even Einstein is an imperfect relativist, and retains Euclidean space and absolute time at the bottom of his calculation, and recovers them at the end, yet the effort to express the system of nature as it would appear from *any* station and to *any* sensorium seems to be eminently enlightening.

Theory and practice in the latest science are still

allied, otherwise neither of them would prosper as it does; but each has taken a leap in its own direction. The distance between them has become greater than the naked eye can measure, and each of them in itself has become unintelligible. We roll and fly at dizzy speeds, and hear at incredible distances; at the same time we imagine and calculate to incredible depths. The technique of science, like that of industry, has become a thing in itself; the one veils its object, which is nature, as the other defeats its purpose, which is happiness. Science often seems to be less the study of things than the study of science. It is now more scholastic than philosophy ever was. We are invited to conceive organisms within organisms, so minute, so free, and so dynamic, that the heart of matter seems to explode into an endless discharge of fireworks, or a mathematical nightmare realised in a thousand places at once, and become the substance of the world. What is even more remarkable—for the notion of infinite organisation has been familiar to the learned at least since the time of Leibniz—the theatre of science is transformed no less than the actors and the play. The upright walls of space, the steady tread of time, begin to fail us; they bend now so obligingly to our perspectives that we no longer seem to travel through them, but to carry them with us, shooting them out or weaving them about us according to some native fatality, which is left unexplained. We seem to have reverted in some sense from Copernicus to Ptolemy: except that the centre is now occupied, not by the solid earth, but by *any* geometrical point chosen for the origin of calculation. Time, too, is not measured by the sun or stars, but by *any* "clock"—that is, by any recurrent rhythm taken as a standard of comparison. It would seem that the existence and energy of each chosen centre, as well as its career and encounters, hang on the collateral existence of other centres of force, among which it must wend its way: yet the only witness to their presence, and the only known property of their substance, is their "radio-activity", or the physical light which they shed. Light, in its physical being, is accordingly the measure of all things in this new philosophy: and if we ask ourselves why this element should have been preferred, the answer is not far to seek. Light is the only medium through which very remote or very minute particles of matter can be revealed to science. Whatever the nature of things may be intrinsically, science must accordingly express the universe in terms of light.

These reforms have come from within: they are triumphs of method. We make an evident advance in logic, and in that parsimony which is dear to philosophers (though not to nature), if we refuse to assign given terms and relations to any prior medium, such as absolute time or space, which cannot be given with them. Observable spaces and times, like the facts observed in them, are given separately and in a desultory fashion. Initially, then, there are as many spaces and times as there are observers, or rather observations; these are the specious times and spaces of dreams, of sensuous life, and of romantic biography. Each is centred here and now, and stretched outwards, forward, and back, as far as imagination has the strength to project it. Then, when objects and events have been posited as self-existent, and when a "clock" and a system of co-ordinates have been established for measuring them, a single mathematical space and time may be deployed about them, conceived to contain all things, and to supply them with their respective places and dates. This gives us the cosmos of classical physics. But this system involves the uncritical notion of light and matter travelling through media previously existing, and being carried down, like a boat drifting down stream, by a flowing time which has a pace of its own, and imposes it on all existence. In reality, each "clock" and each landscape is self-centred and initially absolute: its time and space are irrelevant to those of any other landscape or "clock", unless the objects or events revealed there, being posited as self-existent, actually coincide with those revealed also in another landscape, or dated by another "clock". It is only by travelling along its own path at its own rate that experience or light can ever reach a point lying on another path also, so that two observations, and two measures, may coincide at their ultimate terms, their starting-points or their ends. Positions are therefore not independent of the journey which terminates in them, and thereby individuates them; and dates are not independent of the events which distinguish them. The flux of existence comes first: matter and light distend time by their pulses, they distend space by their deployments.

This, if I understand it, is one half the new theory; the other half is not less acceptable. Newton had described motion as a result of two principles: the first, inertia, was supposed to be inherent in bodies; the second, gravity, was incidental to their co-existence. Yet inherent inertia can only be observed relatively: it makes no difference to me whether I am said to be moving at a great speed or absolutely at rest, if I am not jolted or breathless, and if my felt environment does not change. Inertia, or weight, in so far as it denotes something intrinsic, seems to be but another name for substance or the principle of existence: in so far as it denotes the first law of motion, it seems to be relative to an environment. It would therefore be preferable to combine inertia and attraction in a single formula, expressing the behaviour of bodies towards one another in all their conjunctions, without introducing any inherent forces or absolute measures. This seems to have been done by Einstein, or at least impressively suggested: and it has been found that the new calculations correspond to certain delicate observations more accurately than the old.

This revolution in science seems, then, to be perfectly legal, and ought to be welcomed; yet only under one important moral condition, and with a paradoxical result. The moral condition is that the pride of science should turn into humility, that it should no longer imagine that it is laying bare the intrinsic nature of things. And the paradoxical result is this: that the forms of science are optional, like various languages or methods of notation. One may be more convenient or subtle than another, according to the place, senses, interests, and scope of the explorer; a reform in science may render the old theories antiquated, like the habit of wearing togas, or of going naked; but it cannot render them false, or itself true. Science, when it is more than the gossip of adventure or of experiment, yields practical assurances couched in symbolic terms, but no ultimate insight: so that the intellectual vacancy of the expert, which I was deriding, is a sort of warrant of his solidity. It is rather when the expert prophesies, when he propounds a new philosophy founded on his latest experiments, that we may justly smile at his system, and wait for the next.

Self-knowledge—and the new science is full of self-knowledge—is a great liberator: if perhaps it imposes some retrenchment, essentially it revives courage. Then at last we see what we are and what we can do. The spirit can abandon its vain commitments and false pretensions, like a young man free at last to throw off his clothes and run naked along the sands. Intelligence is never gayer, never surer, than when it is strictly formal, satisfied with the evidence of its materials, as with the lights of jewels, and filled with mounting speculations, as with a sort of laughter. If all the arts aspire to the condition of music, all the sciences aspire to the condition of mathematics. Their logic is their spontaneous and intelligible side: and while they differ from mathematics and from one another in being directed in the first instance upon various unintelligible existing objects, yet as they advance, they unite: because they are everywhere striving to discover in those miscellaneous objects some intelligible order and method. And as the emotion of the pure artist, whatever may be his materials, lies in finding in them some formal harmony or imposing it upon them, so the interest of the scientific mind, in so far as it is free and purely intellectual, lies in tracing their formal pattern. The mathematician can afford to leave to his clients, the engineers, or perhaps the popular philosophers, the emotion of belief: for himself he keeps the lyrical pleasure of metre and of evolving equations: and it is a pleasant surprise to him, and an added problem, if he finds that the arts can use his calculations, or that the senses can verify them; much as if a composer found that the sailors could heave better when singing his songs.

Yet such independence, however glorious inwardly, cannot help diminishing the prestige of the arts in the world. If science misled us before, when it was full of clearness and confidence, how shall we trust it now that it is all mystery and paradox? If classical physics needed this fundamental revision, near to experience and fruitful as it was, what revision will not romantic physics require?

Nor is the future alone insecure: even now the prophets hardly understand one another, or perhaps themselves; and some of them interlard their science with the most dubious metaphysics. Naturally the enemies of science have not been slow to seize this opportunity: the soft-hearted, the muddle-headed, the superstitious are all raising their voices, no longer in desperate resistance to science, but hopefully, and in its name. Science, they tell us, is no longer hostile to religion, or to divination of any sort. Indeed, divination is a science too. Physics is no longer materialistic since space is now curved, and filled with an ether through which light travels at 300,000 kilometres per second—an immaterial rate: because if anything material ventured to move at that forbidden speed, it would be so flattened that it would cease to exist. Indeed, matter is now hardly needed at all; its place has been taken by radio-activity, and by electrons which dart and whirl with such miraculous swiftness, that occasionally, for no known reason, they can skip from orbit to orbit without traversing the intervening positions—an evident proof of free-will in them. Or if solids should still seem to be material, there are astral bodies as well which are immaterial although physical; and as to ether and electricity, they are the very substance of spirit. All this I find announced in newspapers and even in books as the breakdown of scientific materialism: and yet, when was materialism more arrant and barbarous than in these announcements? Something no doubt has broken down: but I am afraid it is rather the habit of thinking clearly and the power to discern the difference between material and spiritual things.

The latest revolution in science will probably not be the last. I do not know what internal difficulties, contradictions, or ominous obscurities may exist in the new theories, or what logical seeds of change, perhaps of radical change, might be discovered there by a competent critic. I base my expectation on two circumstances somewhat more external and visible to the lay mind. One circumstance is that the new theories seem to be affected, and partly inspired, by a particular philosophy, itself utterly insecure. This philosophy regards the point of view as controlling or even creating the object seen; in other words, it identifies the object with the experience or the knowledge of it: it is essentially a subjective, psychological, Protestant philosophy. The study of perspectives, which a severer critic might call illusions, is one of the most interesting and enlightening of studies, and for my own part I should be content to dwell almost exclusively in that poetic and moral atmosphere, in the realm of literature and of humanism. Yet I cannot help seeing that neither in logic nor in natural genesis can perspectives be the ultimate object of science, since a plurality of points of view, somehow comparable, must be assumed in the beginning, as well as common principles of projection, and ulterior points of contact or coincidence. Such assumptions, which must persist throughout, seem to presuppose an absolute system of nature behind all the relative systems of science.

The other circumstance which points to further revolutions is social. The new science is unintelligible to almost all of us; it can be tested only by very delicate observations and very difficult reasoning. We accept it on the authority of a few professors who themselves have accepted it with a contagious alacrity, as if caught in a whirlwind. It has sprung up mysteriously and mightily, like mysticism in a cloister or theology in a council: a Soviet of learned men has proclaimed it. Moreover, it is not merely a system among systems, but a movement among movements. A system, even when it has serious rivals, may be maintained for centuries as religions are maintained, institutionally; but a movement comes to an end; it is followed presently by a period of assimilation which transforms it, or by a movement in some other direction. I ask myself accordingly whether the condition of the world in the coming years will be favourable to refined and paradoxical science. The extension of education will have enabled the uneducated to pronounce upon everything. Will the patronage of capital and enterprise subsist, to encourage discovery and reward invention? Will a jealous and dogmatic democracy respect the unintelligible insight of the few? Will a perhaps starving democracy support materially its Soviet of seers? But let us suppose that no utilitarian fanaticism supervenes, and no intellectual surfeit or discouragement. May not the very profundity of the new science and its metaphysical affinities lead it to bolder developments, inscrutable to the public and incompatible with one another, like the gnostic sects of declining antiquity? Then perhaps that luminous modern thing which until recently was called science, in contrast to all personal philosophies, may cease to exist altogether, being petrified into routine in the practitioners, and fading in the professors into abstruse speculations.

IV

A LONG WAY ROUND TO NIRVANA

That the end of life is death may be called a truism, since the various kinds of immortality that might perhaps supervene would none of them abolish death, but at best would weave life and death together into the texture of a more comprehensive destiny. The end of one life might be the beginning of another, if the Creator had composed his great work like a dramatic poet, assigning successive lines to different characters. Death would then be merely the cue at the end of each speech, summoning the next personage to break in and keep the ball rolling. Or perhaps, as some suppose, all the characters are assumed in turn by a single supernatural Spirit, who amid his endless improvisations is imagining himself living for the moment in this particular solar and social system. Death in such a universal monologue would be but a change of scene or of metre, while in the scramble of a real comedy it would be a change of actors. In either case every voice would be silenced sooner or later, and death would end each particular life, in spite of all possible sequels.

The relapse of created things into nothing is no violent fatality, but something naturally quite smooth and proper. This has been set forth recently, in a novel way, by a philosopher from whom we hardly expected such a lesson, namely Professor Sigmund Freud. He has now broadened his conception of sexual craving or *libido* into a general principle of attraction or concretion in matter, like the Eros of the ancient poets Hesiod and Empedocles. The windows of that stuffy clinic have been thrown open; that smell of acrid disinfectants, those hysterical shrieks, have escaped into the cold night. The troubles of the sick soul, we are given to understand, as well as their cure, after all flow from the stars.

I am glad that Freud has resisted the tendency to represent this principle of Love as the only principle in nature. Unity somehow exercises an evil spell over metaphysicians. It is admitted that in real life it is not well for One to be alone, and

I think pure unity is no less barren and graceless in metaphysics. You must have plurality to start with, or trinity, or at least duality, if you wish to get anywhere, even if you wish to get effectively into the bosom of the One, abandoning your separate existence. Freud, like Empedocles, has prudently introduced a prior principle for Love to play with; not Strife, however (which is only an incident in Love), but Inertia, or the tendency towards peace and death. Let us suppose that matter was originally dead, and perfectly content to be so, and that it still relapses, when it can, into its old equilibrium. But the homogeneous (as Spencer would say) when it is finite is unstable: and matter, presumably not being co-extensive with space, necessarily forms aggregates which have an inside and an outside. The parts of such bodies are accordingly differently exposed to external influences and differently related to one another. This inequality, even in what seems most quiescent, is big with changes, destined to produce in time a wonderful complexity. It is the source of all uneasiness, of life, and of love.

"Let us imagine [writes Freud][1] an undifferentiated vesicle of sensitive substance: then its surface, exposed as it is to the outer world, is by its very position differentiated, and serves as an organ for receiving stimuli.... This morsel of living substance floats about in an outer world which is charged with the most potent energies, and it would be destroyed... if it were not furnished with protection against stimulation. [On the other hand] the sensitive cortical layer has no protective barrier against excitations emanating from within.... The most prolific sources of such excitations are the so-called instincts of the organism.... The child never gets tired of demanding the repetition of a game... he wants always to hear the same story instead of a new one, insists inexorably on exact repetition, and corrects each deviation which the narrator lets slip by mistake.... According to this, *an instinct would be a tendency in living organic matter impelling it towards reinstatement of an earlier condition*, one which it had abandoned under the influence of external disturbing forces—a kind of organic elasticity, or, to put it another way, the manifestation of inertia in organic life.

"If, then, all organic instincts are conservative,

[1] The following quotations are drawn from *Beyond the Pleasure Principle*, by Sigmund Freud; authorised translation by C. J. M. Hubback. The International Psycho-Analytic Press, 1922, pp. 29–48. The italics are in the original.

historically acquired, and directed towards regression, towards reinstatement of something earlier, we are obliged to place all the results of organic development to the credit of external, disturbing, and distracting influences. The rudimentary creature would from its very beginning not have wanted to change, would, if circumstances had remained the same, have always merely repeated the same course of existence.... It would be counter to the conservative nature of instinct if the goal of life were a state never hitherto reached. It must be rather an ancient starting point, which the living being left long ago, and to which it harks back again by all the circuitous paths of development.... *The goal of all life is death.*...

"Through a long period of time the living substance may have...had death within easy reach... until decisive external influences altered in such a way as to compel [it] to ever greater deviations from the original path of life, and to ever more complicated and circuitous routes to the attainment of the goal of death. These circuitous ways to death, faithfully retained by the conservative instincts, would be neither more nor less than the phenomena of life as we know it."

Freud puts forth these interesting suggestions with much modesty, admitting that they are vague and uncertain and (what it is even more important to notice) mythical in their terms; but it seems to me that, for all that, they are an admirable counterblast to prevalent follies. When we hear that there is, animating the whole universe, an *Élan vital*, or general impulse toward some unknown but single ideal, the terms used are no less uncertain, mythical, and vague, but the suggestion conveyed is false—false, I mean, to the organic source of life and aspiration, to the simple naturalness of nature: whereas the suggestion conveyed by Freud's speculations is true. In what sense can myths and metaphors be true or false? In the sense that, in terms drawn from moral predicaments or from literary psychology, they may report the general movement and the pertinent issue of material facts, and may inspire us with a wise sentiment in their presence. In this sense I should say that Greek mythology was true and Calvinist theology was false. The chief terms employed in psycho-analysis have always been metaphorical: "unconscious wishes", "the pleasure-principle", "the Oedipus complex", "Narcissism", "the censor"; nevertheless, interesting and profound vistas may be opened up, in such terms, into the tangle of events in a man's life, and a fresh start may be made with fewer encumbrances and less morbid inhibition. "The shortcomings of our description", Freud says, "would probably disappear if for psychological terms we could substitute physiological or chemical ones. These too only constitute a metaphorical language, but one familiar to us for a much longer time, and perhaps also simpler." All human discourse is metaphorical, in that our perceptions and thoughts are adventitious signs for their objects, as names are, and by no means copies of what is going on materially in the depths of nature; but just as the sportsman's eye, which yields but a summary graphic image, can trace the flight of a bird through the air quite well enough to shoot it and bring it down, so the myths of a wise philosopher about the origin of life or of dreams, though expressed symbolically, may reveal the pertinent movement of nature to us, and may kindle in us just sentiments and true expectations in respect to our fate—for his own soul is the bird this sportsman is shooting.

Now I think these new myths of Freud's about

life, like his old ones about dreams, are calculated to enlighten and to chasten us enormously about ourselves. The human spirit, when it awakes, finds itself in trouble; it is burdened, for no reason it can assign, with all sorts of anxieties about food, pressures, pricks, noises, and pains. It is born, as another wise myth has it, in original sin. And the passions and ambitions of life, as they come on, only complicate this burden and make it heavier, without rendering it less incessant or gratuitous. Whence this fatality, and whither does it lead? It comes from heredity, and it leads to propagation. When we ask how heredity could be started or transmitted, our ignorance of nature and of past time reduces us to silence or to wild conjectures. Something—let us call it matter—must always have existed, and some of its parts, under pressure of the others, must have got tied up into knots, like the mainspring of a watch, in such a violent and unhappy manner that when the pressure is relaxed they fly open as fast as they can, and unravel themselves with a vast sense of relief. Hence the longing to satisfy latent passions, with the fugitive pleasure in doing so. But the external agencies that originally wound up that mainspring never cease to operate; every fresh stimulus gives it another turn, until it snaps, or grows flaccid, or is unhinged. Moreover, from time to time, when circumstances change, these external agencies may encrust that primary organ with minor organs attached to it. Every impression, every adventure, leaves a trace or rather a seed behind it. It produces a further complication in the structure of the body, a fresh charge, which tends to repeat the impressed motion in season and out of season. Hence that perpetual docility or ductility in living substance which enables it to learn tricks, to remember facts, and (when the seeds of past experiences marry and cross in the brain) to imagine new experiences, pleasing or horrible. Every act initiates a new habit and may implant a new instinct. We see people even late in life carried away by political or religious contagions or developing strange vices; there would be no peace in old age, but rather a greater and greater obsession by all sorts of cares, were it not that time, in exposing us to many adventitious influences, weakens or discharges our primitive passions; we are less greedy, less lusty, less hopeful, less generous. But these weakened primitive impulses are naturally by far the strongest and most deeply rooted in the organism: so that although an old man may be converted or may take up some hobby, there is usually something thin in his elderly zeal, compared with the heartiness of youth; nor is it edifying to see a soul in which the plainer human passions are extinct becoming a hotbed of chance delusions.

In any case each fresh habit taking root in the organism forms a little mainspring or instinct of its own, like a parasite; so that an elaborate mechanism is gradually developed, where each lever and spring holds the other down, and all hold the mainspring down together, allowing it to unwind itself only very gradually, and meantime keeping the whole clock ticking and revolving, and causing the smooth outer face which it turns to the world, so clean and innocent, to mark the time of day amiably for the passer-by. But there is a terribly complicated labour going on beneath, propelled with difficulty, and balanced precariously, with much secret friction and failure. No wonder that the engine often gets visibly out of order, or stops short: the marvel is that it ever manages to go at all. Nor is it satisfied with simply revolving and, when at last dismounted, starting afresh in the person of some seed it has dropped, a portion of its substance with all its concentrated instincts wound up tightly within it, and eager to repeat the ancestral experiment; all this growth is not merely material and vain. Each clock in revolving strikes the hour, even the quarters, and often with lovely chimes. These chimes we call perceptions, feelings, purposes, and dreams; and it is because we are taken up entirely with this mental music, and perhaps think that it sounds of itself and needs no music-box to make it, that we find such difficulty in conceiving the nature of our own clocks and are compelled to describe them only musically, that is, in myths. But the ineptitude of our aesthetic minds to unravel the nature of mechanism does not deprive these minds of their own clearness and euphony. Besides sounding their various musical notes, they have the cognitive function of indicating the hour and catching the echoes of distant events or of maturing inward dispositions. This information and emotion, added to incidental pleasures in satisfying our various passions, make up the life of an incarnate spirit. They reconcile it to the external fatality that has wound up the organism, and is breaking it down; and they rescue this organism and all its works from the indignity of being a vain complication and a waste of motion.

That the end of life should be death may sound sad: yet what other end can anything have? The end of an evening party is to go to bed; but its use is to gather congenial people together, that they may pass the time pleasantly. An invitation to the dance is not rendered ironical because the dance cannot last for ever; the youngest of us and the most vigorously wound up, after a few hours, has had enough of sinuous stepping and prancing. The transitoriness of things is essential to their physical being, and not at all sad in itself; it becomes sad by virtue of a sentimental illusion, which makes us imagine that they wish to endure, and that their end is always untimely; but in a healthy nature it is not so. What is truly sad is to have some impulse frustrated in the midst of its career, and robbed of its chosen object; and what is painful is to have an organ lacerated or destroyed when it is still vigorous, and not ready for its natural sleep and dissolution. We must not confuse the itch which our unsatisfied instincts continue to cause with the pleasure of satisfying and dismissing each of them in turn. Could they all be satisfied harmoniously we should be satisfied once for all and completely. Then doing and dying would coincide throughout and be a perfect pleasure.

This same insight is contained in another wise myth which has inspired morality and religion in India from time immemorial: I mean the doctrine of Karma. We are born, it says, with a heritage, a character imposed, and a long task assigned, all due to the ignorance which in our past lives has led us into all sorts of commitments. These obligations we must pay off, relieving the pure spirit within us from its accumulated burdens, from debts and assets both equally oppressive. We cannot disentangle ourselves by mere frivolity, nor by suicide: frivolity would only involve us more deeply in the toils of fate, and suicide would but truncate our misery and leave us for ever a confessed failure. When life is understood to be a process of redemption, its various phases are taken up in turn without haste and without undue attachment; their coming and going have all the keenness of pleasure, the holiness of sacrifice, and the beauty of art. The point is to have expressed and discharged all that was latent in us; and to this perfect relief various temperaments and various traditions assign different names, calling it having one's day, or doing one's duty, or realising one's ideal, or saving one's soul. The task in any case is definite and imposed on us by nature, whether we recognise it or not; therefore we can make true moral progress or fall into real errors. Wisdom and genius lie in discerning this prescribed task and in doing it readily, cleanly, and without distraction. Folly on the contrary imagines that any scent is worth following, that we have an infinite nature, or no nature in particular, that life begins without obligations and can do business without capital, and that the will is vacuously free, instead of being a specific burden and a tight hereditary knot to be unravelled. Some philosophers without self-knowledge think that the variations and further entanglements which the future may bring are the manifestation of spirit; but they are, as Freud has indicated, imposed on living beings by external pressure, and take shape in the realm of matter. It is only after the organs of spirit are formed mechanically that spirit can exist, and can distinguish the better from the worse in the fate of those organs, and therefore in its own fate. Spirit has nothing to do with infinite existence. Infinite existence is something physical and ambiguous; there is no scale in it and no centre. The depths of the human heart are finite, and they are dark only to ignorance. Deep and dark as a soul may be when you look down into it from outside, it is something perfectly natural; and the same understanding that can unearth our suppressed young passions, and dispel our stubborn bad habits, can show us where our true good lies. Nature has marked out the path for us beforehand; there are snares in it, but also primroses, and it leads to peace.

V

THE PRESTIGE OF THE INFINITE

"THE more complex the world becomes and the more it rises above the indeterminate, so much the farther removed it is from God; that is to say, so much the more impious it is." M. Julien Benda[1] is not led to this startling utterance by any political or sentimental grudge. It is not the late war, nor the peace of Versailles, nor the parlous state of the arts, nor the decay of morality and prosperity that disgusts him with our confused world. It is simply overmastering respect for the infinite. *La Trahison des Clercs*, or Treason of the Levites, with which he had previously upbraided the intellectuals of his time, now appears to consist precisely in coveting a part in this world's inheritance, and forgetting that the inheritance of the Levites is the Lord: which, being interpreted

[1] *Essai d'un Discours cohérent sur les Rapports de Dieu et du Monde.* Par Julien Benda. Librairie Gallimard, Paris, 1931.

THE PRESTIGE OF THE INFINITE 103

philosophically, means that a philosopher is bound to measure all things by the infinite.

This infinite is not rhetorical, as if we spoke of infinite thought or infinite love: it is physico-mathematical. Nothing but number, M. Benda tells us, seems to him intelligible. Time, space, volume, and complexity (which appears to the senses as quality) stretch in a series of units, positions, or degrees, to infinity, as number does: and in such homogeneous series, infinite in both directions, there will be no fixed point of origin for counting or surveying the whole and no particular predominant scale. Every position will be essentially identical with every other; every suggested structure will be collapsible and reversible; and the position and relations of every unit will be indistinguishable from those of every other. In the infinite, M. Benda says, the parts have no identity: each number in the scale, as we begin counting from different points of origin, bears also every other number.

This is no mere mathematical puzzle; the thought has a strange moral eloquence. Seen in their infinite setting, which we may presume to be their ultimate environment, all things lose their central position and their dominant emphasis. The contrary of what we first think of them or of ourselves—for instance that we are alive, while they are dead or unborn—is also true. Egotism becomes absurd; pride and shame become the vainest of illusions. If then it be repugnant to reason that the series of numbers, moments, positions, and volumes should be limited—and the human spirit has a great affinity to the infinite—all specific quality and variety in things must be superficial and deeply unreal. They are masks in the carnival of phenomena, to be observed without conviction, and secretly dismissed as ironical by those who have laid up their treasure in the infinite.

This mathematical dissolution of particulars is reinforced by moral considerations which are more familiar. Existence—any specific fact asserting itself in any particular place or moment—is inevitably contingent, arbitrary, gratuitous, and insecure. A sense of insecurity is likely to be the first wedge by which repentance penetrates into the animal heart. If a man did not foresee death and fear it, he might never come at all to the unnatural thought of renouncing life. In fact, he does not often remember death: yet his whole gay world is secretly afraid of being found out, of being foiled in the systematic bluff by which it lives as if its life were immortal; and far more than the brave young man fears death in his own person, the whole life of the world fears to be exorcised by self-knowledge, and lost in air. And with good reason: because, whether we stop to notice this circumstance or not, every fact, every laborious beloved achievement of man or of nature, has come to exist against infinite odds. In the dark grab-bag of Being, this chosen fact was surrounded by innumerable possible variations or contradictions of it; and each of those possibilities, happening not to be realised here and now, yet possesses intrinsically exactly the same aptitude or claim to existence. Nor are these claims and aptitudes merely imaginary and practically contemptible. The flux of existence is continually repenting of its choices, and giving everything actual the lie, by continually substituting something else, no less specific and no less nugatory.

This world, *any* world, exists only by an unmerited privilege. Its glory is offensive to the spirit, like the self-sufficiency of some obstreperous nobody, who happens to have drawn the big prize in a lottery. "The world", M. Benda writes, "inspires me with a double sentiment. I feel it to be full of grandeur, because it has succeeded in asserting itself and coming to exist; and I feel it to be pitiful, when I consider how it hung on a mere nothing that this particular world should never have existed." And though this so accidental world, by its manifold beauties and excitements, may arouse our romantic enthusiasm, it is fundamentally an *unholy* world. Its creation, he adds in italics, "*is something which reason would wish had never taken place*".

For we must not suppose that God, when God is defined as infinite Being, can be the creator of the world. Such a notion would hopelessly destroy that coherence in thought to which M. Benda aspires. The infinite cannot be selective; it cannot possess a particular structure (such, for instance, as the Trinity) nor a particular quality (such as goodness). It cannot exert power or give direction. Nothing can be responsible for the world except the world itself. It has created, or is creating, itself perpetually by its own arbitrary act, by a groundless self-assertion which may be called (somewhat metaphorically) will, or even original sin: the original sin of existence, particularity, selfishness, or separation from God. Existence, being absolutely contingent and ungrounded, is perfectly free: and if it ties itself up in its own habits or laws, and becomes a terrible nightmare to itself by its automatic monotony, that still is only its own work and, figuratively speaking, its own fault. Nothing save its own arbitrary and needless pressure keeps it going in that round. This fatality is impressive, and popular religion has symbolised it in the person of a deity far more often recognised and worshipped than infinite Being. This popular deity, a symbol for the forces of nature and history, the patron of human welfare and morality, M. Benda calls the imperial God.

"It is clear that these two Gods...have nothing to do with one another. The God whom Marshal de Villars, rising in his stirrups and pointing his drawn sword heavenwards, thanks on the evening of Denain, is one God: quite another is the God within whose bosom the author of the *Imitation*, in a corner of his cell, feels the nothingness of all human victories."

It follows from this, if we are coherent, that any "return to God" which ascetic philosophy may bring about cannot be a social reform, a transition to some better form of natural existence in a promised land, a renovated earth, or a material or temporal heaven. Nor can the error of creation be corrected violently by a second arbitrary act, such as suicide, or the annihilation of the universe by some ultimate general collapse. If such events happen, they still leave the door open to new creations and fresh errors. But the marvel is (I will return to this point presently) that the world, in the person of a human individual endowed with reason, may perceive the error of its ways and correct it ideally, in the sphere of estimation and worship. Such is the only possible salvation. Reason, in order to save us, and we, in order to be saved, must both subsist: we must both be incidents in the existing world. We may then, by the operation of reason in us, recover our allegiance to the infinite, for we are bone of its bone and flesh of its flesh: and by our secret sympathy with it we may rescind every particular claim and dismiss silently every particular form of being, as something unreal and unholy.

An even more cogent reason why M. Benda's God cannot have been the creator of the world is that avowedly this God has never existed. We are expressly warned that "if God is infinite Being he excludes existence, in so far as to exist means to be distinct. In the sense which everybody attaches to the word existence, God, as I conceive him, *does not exist*". Of course, in the mind of a lover of the infinite, this fact is not derogatory to God, but derogatory to existence. The infinite remains the first and the ultimate term in thought, the fundamental dimension common to all things, however otherwise they may be qualified; it remains the eternal background against which they all are defined and into which they soon disappear. Evidently, in this divine—because indestructible and necessary—dimension, Being is incapable of making choices, adopting paths of evolution, or exercising power: it knows nothing of phenomena; it is not their cause nor their sanction. It is incapable of love, wrath, or any other passion. "I will add", writes M. Benda, "something else which theories of an impersonal deity have less often pointed out. Since infinity is incompatible with personal being, God is incapable of morality." Thus mere intuition and analysis of the infinite, since this infinite is itself passive and indifferent, may prove a subtle antidote to passion, to folly, and even to life.

I think M. Benda succeeds admirably in the purpose announced in his title of rendering his discourse coherent. If once we accept his definitions, his corollaries follow. Clearly and bravely he disengages his idea of infinity from other properties usually assigned to the deity, such as power, omniscience, goodness, and tutelary functions in respect to life, or to some special human society. But coherence is not completeness, nor even a reasonable measure of descriptive truth; and certain considerations are omitted from M. Benda's view which are of such moment that, if they were included, they might transform the whole issue. Perhaps the chief of these omissions is that of an organ for thought. M. Benda throughout is engaged simply in clarifying his own ideas, and repeatedly disclaims any ulterior pretensions. He finds in the panorama of his thoughts an idea of infinite Being, or God, and proceeds to study the relation of that conception to all others. It is a task of critical analysis and religious confession: and nothing could be more legitimate and, to some of us, more interesting. But whence these various ideas, and whence the spell which the idea of infinite Being in particular casts over the meditative mind? Unless we can view these movements of thought in their natural setting and order of genesis, we shall be in danger of turning autobiography into cosmology and inwardness into folly.

One of the most notable points in M. Benda's analysis is his insistence on the leap involved in passing from infinite Being to any particular fact or system of facts; and again the leap involved in passing, when the converted spirit "returns to God", from specific animal interests—no matter how generous, social, or altruistic these interests may be—to absolute renunciation and sympathy with the absolute. "That a will to return to God should arise in the phenomenal world seems to be a miracle no less wonderful (though it be less wondered at) than that the world should arise in the bosom of God." "Love of man, charity, humanitarianism are nothing but the selfishness of the race, by which each animal species assures its specific existence." "To surrender one's individuality for the benefit of a larger self is something quite different from disinterestedness; it is the exact opposite." And certainly, if we regarded infinite Being as a cosmological medium —say, empty space and time—there would be a miraculous break, an unaccountable new beginning, if that glassy expanse was suddenly wrinkled by something called energy. But in fact there need never have been such a leap, or such a miracle, because there could never have been such a transition. Infinite Being is not a material vacuum "in the bosom" of which a world might arise. It is a Platonic idea—though Plato never entertained it—an essence, non-existent and immutable, not in the same field of reality at all as a world of moving and colliding things. Such an essence is not conceivably the seat of the variations that enliven the world. It is only in thought that we may pass from infinite Being to an existing universe; and when we turn from one to the other, and say that now energy has emerged from the bosom of God, we are turning over a new leaf, or rather picking up an entirely different volume. The natural world is composed of objects and events which theory may regard as transformations of a hypothetical energy; an energy which M. Benda—who when he comes down to the physical world is a good materialist—conceives to have condensed and distributed itself into matter, which in turn composed organisms and ultimately generated consciousness and reason. But in whatever manner the natural world may have evolved, it is found and posited by us in perception and action, not, like infinite Being, defined in thought. This contrast is ontological, and excludes any derivation of the one object from the other. M. Benda himself tells us so; and we may wonder why he introduced infinite Being at all into his description of the world. The reason doubtless is that he was not engaged in describing the world, except by the way, but rather in classifying and clarifying his ideas in view of determining his moral allegiance. And he arranged his terms, whether ideal or material, in a single series, because they were alike present to his intuition, and he was concerned to arrange them in a hierarchy, according to their moral dignity.

Not only is infinite Being an incongruous and obstructive term to describe the substance of the world (which, if it subtends the changes in the world and causes them, must evidently change with them), but even mathematical space and time, in their ideal infinity, may be very far from describing truly the medium and groundwork of the universe. That is a question for investigation and hypothesis, not for intuition. But in the life of intuition, when that life takes a mathematical turn, empty space and time and their definable structure may be important themes; while, when the same life becomes a discipline of the affections, we see by this latest example, as well as by many a renowned predecessor of M. Benda, that infinite Being may dominate the scene.

Nor is this eventual dominance so foreign to

the natural mind, or such a miraculous conversion, as it might seem. Here, too, there is no derivation of object from object, but an alternative for the mind. As M. Benda points out, natural interests and sympathies may expand indefinitely, so as to embrace a family, a nation, or the whole animate universe; we might even be chiefly occupied with liberal pursuits, such as science or music; the more we laboured at these things and delighted in them, the less ready should we be for renunciation and detachment. Must conversion then descend upon us from heaven like a thunderbolt? Far from it. We need not look for the principle of spiritual life in the distance: we have it at home from the beginning. Even the idea of infinite Being, though unnamed, is probably familiar. Perhaps in the biography of the human race, or of each budding mind, the infinite or indeterminate may have been the primary datum. On that homogeneous sensuous background, blank at first but secretly plastic, a spot here and a movement there may gradually have become discernible, until the whole picture of nature and history had shaped itself as we see it. A certain sense of that primitive datum, the infinite or indeterminate, may always remain as it were the outstretched canvas on which every picture is painted. And when the pictures vanish, as in deep sleep, the ancient simplicity and quietness may be actually recovered, in a conscious union with Brahma. So sensuous, so intimate, so unsophisticated the "return to God" may be for the spirit, without excluding the other avenues, intellectual and ascetic, by which this return may be effected in waking life, though then not so much in act as in intent only and allegiance.

I confess that formerly I had some difficulty in sharing the supreme respect for infinite Being which animates so many saints: it seemed to me the dazed, the empty, the deluded side of spirituality. Why rest in an object which can be redeemed from blank negation only by a blank intensity? But time has taught me not to despise any form of vital imagination, any discipline which may achieve perfection after any kind. Intuition is a broadly based activity; it engages elaborate organs and sums up and synthesises accumulated impressions. It may therefore easily pour the riches of its ancestry into the image or the sentiment which it evokes, poor as this sentiment or image might seem if expressed in words. In rapt or ecstatic moments, the vital momentum, often the moral escape, is everything, and the achievement, apart from that blessed relief, little or nothing. Infinite Being may profit in this way by offering a contrast to infinite annoyance. Moreover, in my own way, I have discerned in pure Being the involution of all forms. As felt, pure Being may be indeterminate, but as conceived reflectively it includes all determinations: so that when deployed into the realm of essence, infinite or indeterminate Being truly contains entertainment for all eternity.

M. Benda feels this pregnancy of the infinite on the mathematical side; but he hardly notices the fact, proclaimed so gloriously by Spinoza, that the infinity of extension is only one of an infinity of infinites. There is an aesthetic infinite, or many aesthetic infinites, composed of all the forms which nature or imagination might exhibit; and where imagination fails, there are infinite remainders of the unimagined. The version which M. Benda gives us of infinite Being, limited to the mathematical dimension, is therefore unnecessarily cold and stark. His one infinity is monochrome, whereas the total infinity of essence, in which an infinity of outlines is only one item, is infinitely many-coloured. Phenomena therefore fall, in their essential variety, within and not without infinite Being: so that in "returning to God" we might take the whole world with us, not indeed in its blind movement and piecemeal illumination, as events occur, but in an after-image and panoramic portrait, as events are gathered together in the realm of truth.

On the whole I think M. Benda's two Gods are less unfriendly to one another than his aggrieved tone might suggest. This pregnant little book ends on a tragic note.

"Hitherto human self-assertion in the state or the family, while serving the imperial God, has paid some grudging honours, at least verbally, to the infinite God as well, under the guise of liberalism, love of mankind, or the negation of classes. But today this imperfect homage is retracted, and nothing is reverenced except that which gives strength. If anyone preaches human kindness, it is in order to establish a "strong" community martially trained, like a super-state, to oppose everything not included within it, and to become omnipotent in the art of utilising the non-human forces of nature.... The will to return to God may prove to have been, in the history of the phenomenal world, a sublime accident."

Certainly the will to "return to God", if not an accident, is an incident in the life of the world; and the whole world itself is a sublime accident, in the sense that its existence is contingent, groundless, and precarious. Yet so long as the imperial God continues successfully to keep our world going, it will be no accident, but a natural necessity, that many a mind should turn to the thought of the infinite with awe, with a sense of liberation, and even with joy. The infinite God owes all his worshippers, little as he may care for them, to the success of the imperial God in creating reflective and speculative minds. Or (to drop these mythological expressions which may become tiresome) philosophers owe to nature and to the discipline of moral life their capacity to look beyond nature and beyond morality. And while they may *look* beyond, and take comfort in the vision, they cannot *pass* beyond. As M. Benda says, the most faithful Levite can return to the infinite only in his thought; in his life he must remain a lay creature. Yet nature, in forming the human soul, unintentionally unlocked for the mind the doors to truth and to essence, partly by obliging the soul to attend to things which are outside, and partly by endowing the soul with far greater potentialities of sensation and invention than daily life is likely to call forth. Our minds are therefore naturally dissatisfied with their lot and speculatively directed upon an outspread universe in which our persons count for almost nothing. These insights are calculated to give our brutal wills some pause. Intuition of the infinite and recourse to the infinite for religious inspiration follow of themselves, and can never be suppressed altogether, so long as life is conscious and experience provokes reflection.

Spirit is certainly not one of the forces producing spirit, but neither is it a contrary force. It is the actuality of feeling, of observation, of meaning. Spirit has no unmannerly quarrel with its parents, its hosts, or even its gaolers: they know not what they do. Yet spirit belongs intrinsically to another sphere, and cannot help wondering at the world, and suffering in it. The man in whom spirit is awake will continue to live and act, but with a difference. In so far as he has become pure spirit he will have transcended the fear of death or defeat; for now his instinctive fear, which will subsist, will be neutralised by an equally sincere consent to die and to fail. He will live henceforth in a truer and more serene sympathy with nature than is possible to rival natural beings. Natural beings are perpetually struggling to live only, and not to die; so that their will is in hopeless rebellion against the divine decrees which they must obey notwithstanding. The spiritual man, on the contrary, in so far as he has already passed intellectually into the eternal world, no longer endures unwillingly the continual death involved in living, or the final death involved in having been born. He renounces everything religiously in the very act of attaining it, resigning existence itself as gladly as he accepts it, or even more gladly; because the emphasis which action and passion lend to the passing moment seems to him arbitrary and violent; and as each task or experience is dismissed in turn, he accounts the end of it more blessed than the beginning.

CAMBRIDGE: PRINTED BY
W. LEWIS, M.A.
AT THE UNIVERSITY PRESS